THE
SUBURBANIST

Also by Geoff Nicholson

The Miranda
The London Complaint
The City Under the Skin
Walking in Ruins
The Lost Art of Walking
Gravity's Volkswagen
Sex Collectors
The Hollywood Dodo
Bedlam Burning
Female Ruins
Flesh Guitar
Bleeding London
Footsucker
Everything and More
Still Life with Volkswagens
The Errol Flynn Novel
Day Trips to the Desert
The Food Chain
Hunters and Gatherers
Big Noises
What We Did on Our Holidays
The Knot Garden
Street Sleeper

THE
SUBURBANIST

A Personal Account
and Ambivalent Celebration
of Life in the Suburbs,
with Field Notes

GEOFF NICHOLSON

Harbour

First published by Harbour in 2021
Harbour Books (East) Ltd, PO Box 10594
Chelmsford, Essex CM1 9PB
info@harbourbooks.co.uk

A CIP catalogue record for this book is available from the British Library

ISBN 978 1905128 327

Typeset by Tetragon, London
Printed and bound in Great Britain by Clays Ltd, Elcograf S.p.A

Contents

The Necessary Pandemic Preface

I started writing this book a couple of years ago, after a couple of decades thinking about it. An early draft was completed right before the arrival of the Covid 19 virus, though there was still work to be done. I believed, perhaps naively, perhaps arrogantly, that I wasn't a candidate for the 'worst-case scenario'. I might possibly catch the virus, but I didn't expect to die or to have a long, painful illness. I didn't expect to lose my job because I was a freelance writer and didn't have a job to lose.

Like everyone else, I could see that life would change; I'd have my travel plans ruined, my social life put on hold, my shopping habits severely modified, but at the start of the pandemic I wanted to believe it would be business as usual for me as a writer. I would continue to do what I always did. I would stay at home (which had suddenly become a government imperative) and I would write. There would be various other home-centred activities: reading, watching films, listening to music, improving my patchy musical skills, messing about in the garden, emerging from time to time for what had been decreed a permissible daily walk, which on some days included a detour to the local super-market to buy food. But these were all the things I did anyway.

It wasn't exciting or dramatic, but it was the life I was accus-tomed to, and to a great extent had created for myself. It was odd to think that because of a lockdown, because of what turned out to be a cascade of lockdowns, a lot of people in Britain would suddenly be conducting their lives very much the way I'd been doing for a long time as a writer. It must have come as a ter-rible shock to most of them. And if they experienced heightened levels of isolation, loneliness, anxiety and depression, well that was all part of the package. A study from Manchester University concluded that the pandemic did not lead to an increase in suicides, though it's well documented that it led to an increase in domestic violence.

It so happened that at the time Covid arrived I was a single man, recently and unhappily divorced, recently returned to England after a decade and a half in California, living alone in suburbia in Essex: I still am and still do. I didn't move to the suburbs because I thought it would be safe: I moved there because it was comparatively cheap. And although the inhabit-ants of suburbia were obviously not immune to coronavirus or to the changes it created, it was widely said that the pandemic was much more bearable, much more survivable, if you lived in the suburbs.

There was no great mystery about this. Social distancing is easier when you have some actual distance between you and your neighbours. Since most suburbanites have their own patch of garden they were less likely to feel locked up and cooped up than if they'd been living, say, in a small flat in an inner city.

When they took that daily, government-sanctioned walk they were able to find some suburban green space.

There was one enormous change, and perhaps benefit, for many suburb dwellers: they were encouraged, in some cases forced, not just to stay at home, but to work from home, just like I did. Whatever else this involved, it meant they didn't have to commute. It led to a major reduction in hours spent travelling, less time on trains, buses, and the Underground, in close proximity to others. At the height of the first lockdown, there were days when the newly extended car park at my local suburban station, which in general can and does accommodate many hundred vehicles, was occupied by just three; subsequent lockdowns and variations on a lockdown never saw so few.

The media were quick to pick up on this change in working patterns. Journalists with space and word counts to fill, began to sing the praises of suburbia. The *Spectator* ran an article by Ross Clark headlined: 'Could coronavirus make suburbia cool again?' You might have countered with Betteridge's Law of Headlines: 'Any headline that ends in a question mark can be answered by the word no.' I would also doubt that use of the word 'again'. Was suburbia *ever* cool? But Clark's idea of coolness was largely about property values. He wrote,

> Don't be surprised if the property market's big winners from coronavirus are family homes with good-sized gardens either in the suburbs or in rural locations with excellent broadband and reasonably close to main towns and cities. If you have a fear of all this happening again, it makes sense to invest in a lockdown-proof property – possibly flogging the city-centre flat and rural bolthole to invest in a single suburban home where you could happily hide away for a few weeks or months. Not for years has Tom and Barbara's place in Surbiton seemed so attractive.

It seemed to me this was unlikely to be a widespread or long-term trend: just how many people actually have both a city-centre flat and a rural bolthole to sell? But it was nice to see the reference to Tom and Barbara from the 1970s sitcom *The Good Life*. Some suburban cultural touchstones are uncannily enduring.

In *The Times* there was an article by Carol Lewis titled 'The Top 20 Suburbs in the UK'. Quidgeley, near Gloucester, was top of a table labelled 'suburbs growing fastest in popularity', with a 47% increase in 'interested buyers', although some of the data was collected pre-Covid. A passage in the article ran, 'there is nothing outdated about the suburbs – now that city centres lie silent, it is where the young aspire to be.' I haven't conducted a survey of 'the young' (I suspect Carol Lewis hasn't either) but that doesn't quite ring true to me. My own suburb didn't make that list, though homes continued to be bought and sold throughout the pandemic, which surprised me.

I decided not to keep a 'Covid Diary', partly because I thought that anybody with a laptop and even the vaguest literary inclinations would be doing that, but more because I reckoned that when the time came to write about it later, i.e. now, the things I couldn't remember were probably not worth remembering, and if certain things seemed a blur or non-sequential, then that was all part of the experience.

I clearly remember, for instance, very early in the first lockdown, speaking to one of my neighbours who owns a floppy, likeable hound with lovely mottled fur, and I said, 'Ah he doesn't even know there's anything going on.' The neighbour agreed, saying, 'Yes, as long as he gets fed and has three walks a day he's happy.' Yes, three walks a day did strike me as a lot. But later I thought that maybe some of the local animals *did* detect that something was going on. At the very least they must have seen that in the early days there was next to no traffic. Cats roamed the streets as if they owned them, and even pigeons and magpies walked blithely across the tarmacked roads. As the lockdown progressed and there were increasing numbers of cars, there was also a corresponding increase in roadkill, not just birds but also hares and hedgehogs. I suppose the critters had rapidly been lulled into a false sense of security, but they just as rapidly returned to their old, cautious ways.

As I did my suburban walks in those early days, it appeared that everyone was at home. All the driveways were full of cars, as though they'd come home to roost. The majority always looked newly washed. However, one day, a little way up the street, there was a car parked half in the road, half on the pavement, its front and driver's side smashed in, with debris and oil all over the road. The received wisdom was that the roads were so empty some people were now driving like maniacs.

Naturally, as I walked I saw other people walking, far more than usual, people who often swerved to avoid me in order to stay the regulation six feet away, and sometimes they went so far as to cross the road. Some of them were good humoured about it, some not. When the second and subsequent lockdowns and quasi-lockdowns came, people gave each other much less room.

I remember when rainbows started appearing in the front windows of some of the houses: kids' drawings and paintings, some done freehand, others coloured-in on preprinted sheets of paper. I swear I had no idea what this was about. I thought it couldn't really be celebrating a rainbow coalition of sexual difference and diversity, and it took me perhaps longer than it should have to work out that this was a way of thanking the National Health Service. Those were the days when we tried to save the NHS by not using it, the way you might limit the depreciation of a car by never driving it.

I remember spending a lot of time engaged in that ultra-suburban activity of staring out of the window to see what my neighbours were up to. I couldn't see all that much but I learned which neighbour had a trampoline, which had a portable above-ground swimming pool. I think I saw love blossom between a couple of older, single, isolated neighbours, but that may have been wishful thinking. I saw a lot of people running and jogging, many of them out-of-shape men who had decided to take this opportunity to get fit. A surprising number wore tight unflattering outfits as if to remind themselves just how much work they had to do. I saw fewer and fewer of them as time went by.

I also saw quite a few couples on foot, each carrying a big bag of groceries. I'd never seen that before. I supposed that, like me, they were combining their shopping and their exercise. It seemed it could have been a bonding activity that brought the people closer together, though I can't say they ever looked very happy or united. But on balance the suburbanites did their best: they tended their gardens, they started DIY projects, they took up new hobbies, improved their baking or embroidery, tried learning a new language, tried to home-school their children, all harmless, self-contained occupations, and no doubt by some standards insufferably suburban. I suppose it would have been possible to live in the suburbs, attend illegal raves and become a superspreader, but I don't believe this is what many, if any, suburbanites did.

And then one day I looked out of my window and saw a man and a woman walking down the street, my street, in full *Star Wars* stormtrooper gear, armoured, masked and brandishing what I trust was fake weaponry. It did seem a bit excessive as personal protective equipment against the virus, and given the way they waved at passers-by I assumed it had to be a stunt for charity. Only later did I realise the day was May 4th as in 'May the fourth be with you.' I imagine this pair might have walked along my street dressed like that on any May 4th whether there'd been a pandemic or not, but the lockdown did give it some extra poignancy.

The Queen sent us all a message, saying that the streets were not empty, but filled with love. I really wasn't sure about that.

The streets I walked in seemed increasingly filled with simmering, suppressed rage. I remember saying, when we didn't know how long we were going to be locked down, 'If this goes on for too long there'll be rioting and looting.' I wasn't the only person saying this, and it turned out we were all correct, if not exactly in the way we anticipated.

We needed an American example to follow. After the killing in Minneapolis of George Floyd (who was black) by a policeman (who was white) many parts of the United States erupted in protests that frequently turned violent. This included Los Angeles, where I had lived when I was married, before my divorce, immediately before coming back to the English suburbs. There were pictures of tanks on a section of Hollywood Boulevard where I had regularly walked and driven. Inevitably I wondered how things would have been if I'd still been living in LA, and it was strange to think that I was locked down in England while my ex-wife was locked down in the American house in the American suburb where we'd once lived together.

Black Lives Matter – both the slogan and the organisation – returned front and centre, and England had its own version of civil unrest, its own anti-racism demonstrations, one symptom of which was the toppling of statues of real and/or imagined imperialists and racists. I don't doubt the sincerity and genuine feeling of many of the protestors, but even so there was a sense that much of this unrest, its vehemence and destructiveness, was displacement activity for other kinds of discontent.

Of course none of this mayhem happened in my own suburb, or in any other English suburb that I'm aware of. In my suburb we have a few 'black lives' but we don't have any statues. The only bit of looting I saw anywhere in the vicinity came when the glass front door of the nearby Boots was smashed in. The word on the street was that it had been done as part of a raid to steal paracetamol, which was in short supply at the time, and could supposedly be sold on eBay at a mighty premium.

It sounded plausible though I had no idea if it was true. A couple of months later the plate-glass window of the local wine bar was smashed by what the papers referred to simply as vandals, thereby suggesting no racial or political motive, and when I talked to the owner of the wine bar it didn't seem that anything had been looted. I assume the police were called to both these crime scenes, and I assume they did what they were supposed to do, but it's very rare indeed to see a policeman in these parts. That's arguably one of the attractions of suburban life.

The American politician Alexandria Ocasio-Cortez apparently agrees. She's the young (well, young for a politician) Democrat Representative for the New York 14th district. In the wake of the American troubles, there were calls in the US to 'defund the police' – a very misleading name for a reasonable proposition. It didn't simply mean to take all funding away from the police, leaving them with just a truncheon and a whistle, but rather it envisaged a better use of resources. Instead of spending ever more money to beef up policing, the answer might be to reallocate some of that money to social projects that could benefit the whole community, reduce crime and therefore make less policing necessary.

Ocasio-Cortez was asked on Twitter: 'What does an America with defunded police look like to you?' and she replied, 'It looks like a suburb.' As you can imagine, I choked on my ambrosia salad when I read that. She went on (the punctuation, spelling, abbreviations and capitals are hers, or Twitter's),

> Affluent white communities already live in a world where they choose to fund youth, health, housing etc more than they fund police. These communities have lower crime rates not because they have more police, but because they have more resources to support healthy society in a way that reduces crime.

When a teen or a preteen does something harmful in a suburb (I say teen because this is often when lifelong carceral cycles begin for Black and Brown communities). White communities bend over backwards to find alternatives to incarceration for their loved ones to 'protect their future', like community service or rehab or restorative measures. Why don't we treat Black and Brown people the same way?

Affluent White suburbs also design their own lives so that they walk through the world without having much interrupt or interaction with police at all, aside from community events and speeding tickets.

You could counter with a few ifs and buts, but the idea seems basically a good one. It also sounds as though Ocasio-Cortez thinks the suburbs are *a good thing*. This places her in a strange relation to most leftist politics, where the suburbs haven't been 'approved of' since about 1948. Praise for the suburbs has always been the province of American conservatives.

Donald Trump, somewhat later, also chipped in his ten cents worth: the time of Covid was, of course, also the time of his second presidential run. He tweeted,

> I am happy to inform all of the people living their Suburban Lifestyle Dream that you will no longer be bothered or financially hurt by having low income housing built in your neighborhood … Your housing prices will go up based on the market, and crime will go down. I have rescinded the Obama-Biden AFFH Rule. Enjoy!

Had anybody before Trump ever used the term 'Suburban Lifestyle Dream'? If so, I've been unable to find evidence. In any case, AFFH stands for Affirmatively Furthering Fair Housing, a programme from the Obama administration intended to make

American suburbs more diverse. The rule, which came into force in 2015, required cities and towns that received federal funding to spot patterns of racial bias in their local housing and take corrective action. Trump no doubt was playing to what he imagined was his constituency, stirring up social and racial anxieties among suburbanites, stoking the fear of having cheap social housing built on their doorstep. He believed this was a vote-catcher. He may have been right, but anti-Trump commentators said he was peddling an outdated notion of what the American suburbs were actually like, that white suburbanites no longer lived in fear of non-whites moving in, because many already had, and the all-white, closed-minded suburbia of legend no longer existed. It would be nice to think Trump was wrong about current suburban anxieties as about so much else, but perhaps he detected that the real worry in suburbia is not about social and racial change as about falling house prices, though I don't imagine that anybody anywhere is exactly thrilled when they learn the value of their property has gone down.

Did the pandemic affect what I've written in this book? Well yes, to some extent, otherwise I wouldn't be writing this preface. For one thing, if it hadn't been for Covid, the book would have been finished, published and out there finding its audience considerably sooner, though I'm well aware that this is one of the more minor tragedies caused by the pandemic. The delay at least gave me time for another couple of field trips, conducted between lockdowns, and there were opportunities for second and third thoughts about what I'd already written, time for making new discoveries. For example, it was during this period that I became a fan of the waspish suburban joys of Barbara Pym's fiction.

This comparatively short passage of time has also given new perspectives to certain things I'd already written. My chapter on the suburbs of Sheffield mentions Peter Sutcliffe, the Yorkshire Ripper, who was alive and serving a whole-life prison sentence in HMP Frankland at the time I wrote it. He was caught by police in the suburb of Broomhill, in a road behind my old school. While I was editing and re-editing the manuscript, he died in hospital of coronavirus, having refused treatment. It's hard to see anything noble about this, but I'm sure I'm just one of the many people who was glad enough that Sutcliffe didn't use up too many of the NHS's scarce resources before he passed on. Jan Morris, who had some interesting things to say about Australian suburbia, also died during the pandemic, aged 94, but her death was not so widely covered.

Also, after Covid, we read some things differently. My text mentions the plague, a feature and plot device of Boccaccio's *Decameron* and Ben Jonson's *The Alchemist*, causing certain characters to move to the suburbs to avoid contagion. When I first wrote that section of the book, plague seemed a distant, unreal phenomenon, perhaps a literary conceit. It doesn't feel that way now.

There's evidence, much talked up during the pandemic, that Shakespeare wrote the poems *Venus and Adonis* and *The Rape of Lucrece* as well as the plays *Antony and Cleopatra*, *Macbeth* and *King Lear* during various outbreaks of the plague, while the Globe was shuttered and he was in isolation. You could conclude it was an ill-wind.

You could also perhaps take some consolation from knowing that Shakespeare survived, that the plague, without the benefit of modern science and modern politicians, did eventually recede. Many people lived through it and came out the other side, not untouched but intact. And while the Black Death may not be much on everybody's mind these days, there are still plenty of things other than coronavirus that we might be worried about. We haven't been able to eradicate flu or pneumonia, and people die of them all the time, but we've found a way of living with them, incorporating the risks and worries into our version of normality.

That's what we wanted all through the Covid pandemic. As we clipped our hedges, baked our banana bread, practised with our theremins, we were well aware that these too were displacement activities, coping mechanisms. We didn't want to die, but neither did we want to be prevented from seeing our loved ones, earning a living, going to restaurants, the football match, the local charity shop. We authors didn't want our books to remain unfinished, unpublished, unread. We wanted the pandemic to be over so we could return to normal or even a new normal. We wanted a *vaccine*, maybe more than one.

Right at the beginning of the pandemic, well before the first lockdown, I happened to be speaking to my own doctor about other matters. As I left he advised me to avoid crowded pubs and if I happened to be in London and was thinking about taking the Tube for a couple of stops then I should walk instead. This sounded like advice I could follow, and I said, 'So what we're really doing here is just trying to hunker down until somebody comes up with a vaccine, is that it?' He didn't quite say yes but he didn't say no either. Nor did he say, as he might have, 'Don't hold your breath.'

But eventually vaccines came. There were, and are, several to choose from, promising a return to something resembling normality in three or six or twelve months. We were told to be take nothing for granted but to be optimistic, though it was perfectly possible to take nothing for granted and be *pessimistic*. Big Pharma, until then widely understood to be an unalloyed evil, was involved in the development of all of them. The vaccine names, to an Anglophone, sounded alien and exotic and not especially friendly: Moderna, Novavax, Valneva, GSK/Sanofi Pasteur, Oxford/AstraZeneca, Janssen. Wouldn't it have been possible to come up with some more benign, more domestic, possibly more *suburban* names? The Conservatory Vaccine, The Double Glazed-Vaccine? The Crazy Paving Vaccine?

The nearest we came to domesticity was the Pfizer/BioNtech vaccine, which didn't sound especially homely in itself, but it was developed by a German-Turkish married couple, Ugat Sahin and Ozlem Tureci who, by all accounts, were driven by altruism not profit, even though their company stood to make a few billion dollars from their research. We read how they worked hard, lived modestly, rode bicycles. I so wanted them to live in a nice little semi in the suburbs, but in fact, being good solid Europeans, they lived in a flat, in the city of Mainz, on the Rhine.

As I write these words, it appears that vaccines will, sooner rather than later, be available and will enable us to control the coronavirus. It might be nice to think that the pandemic has changed us radically and permanently, turned us into kinder, gentler, more compassionate people, with a greater understanding of life and mortality, but which of us would be arrogant or foolish enough to make those claims for ourselves?

For most of us it's a return to our all-too-ordinary lives, lives made up of small, quotidian matters, which in the greater scheme of things may not add up to much, but it seems to me that if we're lucky life is mostly made up of small, quotidian matters, and not only in suburbia. Life in the suburbs is much condemned for being too tame, too predictable, too commonplace, but there are times, say in the middle of a pandemic, when it seems that the tame, the predictable and the commonplace are what we live for, the very things that keep us sane and allow us to survive. They're the very things that can save us.

GEOFF NICHOLSON
Essex, January 2021

1

Native in Suburbia

Sometimes I ask myself what I'm doing here. 'Here' in this case being my small two-bedroom house in the suburban enclave of Lawford Dale, one of a cluster of separate suburban developments outside Manningtree, in Essex. These suburbs are of different ages, different degrees of style and expense. Up the hill is Summers Park, 'luxurious 3,4 &5-bedroom homes' and across the road from there is Lawford Place, a suburb that was formerly a manor house, then the research department of BX Plastics where Margaret Thatcher worked briefly, commuting from Colchester. That place is about as ritzy as any suburb I've ever seen.

If developers had had their way, there would also be any number of other suburbs built on local green-field sites.

Developers draw up plans, there are protests of varying degrees of vehemence, pretty much always done in the name of conservation though with a definite overtone of Nimbyism, a few get through, many don't. Even so, if you add up the numbers you'll calculate that more people live in Lawford, the *suburb*, than live in Manningtree, the *urb*.

Obviously this doesn't answer the question of why I'm here. One simple, although no doubt partial, explanation is that I arrived here a few years ago, emotionally shell-shocked from a bad, painful and unexpected divorce. (Not my idea: I hadn't even known we had a problem, which I now suppose was part of the problem. My wife and I had been together for twenty years, the last fifteen of those in Los Angeles, by some accounts the most suburban city on earth, though not in quite the way that English cities are.) I came back to England, looked around me, found Lawford Dale and thought, yes, OK this will do.

My wife and I had split the money from the sale of the (yes, suburban) house in LA. I wanted to live in London, but the amount of money I had couldn't buy anything I'd have wanted to live in. The cost of a house in Lawford was about half of any one-bedroom flat I could have bought in London. The choice wasn't a difficult one. I wasn't tired of London, I just couldn't afford to live there. Would I rather have moved into a luxury penthouse overlooking the Thames? Well of course I would. For that matter, I would have preferred to be happily married and still living with my wife in a suburban house in Los Angeles. But since neither of these options was remotely possible, I found myself here, making the best of it.

I realise that I've spent large parts of my life living in very different kinds of suburb, in England and in the United States. And although it was never a project, could never have been thought of as 'research', I've wandered around and explored, and sometimes photographed, the suburbs of Toronto, Tokyo, Marrakesh, Melbourne, Palm Springs and plenty of other places, wherever I happened to find myself. There was nothing systematic about it, but I was consistent, and often I preferred it to seeing the great sights, the great attractions, even places of great natural or man-made beauty. I wasn't being perverse, I was simply fascinated by the ordinary, quotidian places and spaces where so many people live. I was fascinated by the houses and garages and gardens, the sheer ordinariness, the ways in which people had or hadn't expressed their individuality, the ways that people had conformed or rejected conformity. I always liked to think of myself as an outsider, a detached (or perhaps semi-detached) observer, a low-level anthropologist in search of the tribes of suburbia. But in reality I had already gone native.

Look, I'm not naive, I know that the suburbs get a bad rap, not only as a physical place but as a state of mind and a set of ideals. Of course the haters, whom I'll discuss at length later, will say these states of mind, these ideals, are of a numbing, anaesthetised, conventional, conservative or emotionally stunted kind, but these afflictions are hardly restricted to suburbia. It may amaze certain readers but some of the people in vibrant urban centres, or for that matter, idyllic rural places, can be all these things too. The apologists, and I don't actually consider myself an apologist since I don't think I have anything to apologise for, will say that the suburban ideal is about decency, being house-proud, being a responsible parent, being a good neighbour, and in part it is, although again I realise that these things are not restricted to suburbia either.

Also I'm not Pollyanna-ish about any of this. I see the faults and the failings of suburbia. Of course much of the architecture is dull, some of the people too, but I think there are far worse things to be than dull. And once again, I don't believe the suburbs have a monopoly on dull architecture and dull people.

And neither am I a knee-jerk contrarian. I don't like things simply because so many other people dislike them, but I'm interested in why so many people put so much energy and vitriol into denouncing the suburbs. Is it real? Is it a pose? Is it based on experience, or lack of it? I'm sure it says something about the suburbs that they have so many detractors, and it surely says something about the detractors themselves. To insist that you hate the suburbs may be a way of asserting that you're a superior kind of being, that you aren't a suburbanite, you're a metropolitan, a cosmopolitan, an urbanist, an internationalist, a Bohemian. Friend, there's something really, really *suburban* about that.

Lawford Dale, 'my suburb' as I increasingly come to think of it, is located a short, easy walk from the centre of Manningtree, the smallest market town in England, once a port, rugged enough to have had a brothel and a horse skinnery. My suburb is even closer to the River Stour estuary: a wide expanse of water if the tide is in, a wide expanse of mud if it's out, though it can be spectacularly beautiful either way. There's also, just in case you think things are getting a bit cutesy, a small industrial estate with car dismantlers, self-storage units and a factory that manufactures food additives. Even Dedham Vale, Constable country, is only a few miles away. However, being the subversive that I am, I often prefer to concentrate on the delights and eccentricities of the suburb itself.

Lawford Dale was built on what had been agricultural land by Hey and Croft, a developer based in nearby Witham. Work started in the 1980s but Hey and Croft went bust in 1992. The development was planned for eighty-nine 'residential terraced, semi-detached houses and chalet bungalows'. I think my house must be one of those 'chalet bungalows', though it doesn't strike me as being much of a chalet – a word that invokes the Swiss Alps and/or Butlin's holiday camps – and it definitely isn't a bungalow since it has an upstairs that's almost as big as the downstairs, but who would ever trust developer-speak when it comes to architectural definitions? In fact there are no bungalows per se in Lawford Dale itself, which surprised me;

the bungalow seems to be such a suburban mainstay, though there are some bungalows down the hill by the main road, just outside Lawford Dale proper.

The street names in Lawford Dale invoke great English artists: you'll find Turner Avenue, Gainsborough Drive, Blake Close, Constable Close, Nash Close, Hughes-Stanton Way. If that last one seems obscure, its refers to Blair Hughes-Stanton, a local artist who was very successful and accomplished in his day, if not currently well known. His daughter – Penny Hughes-Stanton – runs a serious art gallery in Manningtree. See, we are not all Philistines in this part of suburbia.

There's also Keating Drive, which I assume was named after Tom Keating, the briefly infamous art forger who died a few years before the building of the estate began. A fine example of developer's humour there. There are also one or two streets that don't seem to be named after visual artists – Fitzgerald and Sitwell, for instance. I wonder if the builders had run through all the artists they could think of and moved on to writers. Or was it that their knowledge of artists was far more encyclopedic than mine, so that the streets may be named in honour of, say, John Anster Fitzgerald (a Victorian 'fairy painter') and some obscure watercolourist from the Sitwell clan of whom I've never heard.

The houses in Lawford Dale aren't fancy but they're not entirely run-of-the-mill. The walls are generally red and yellow brick, which are facings of course; behind the bricks are standard breeze blocks. A few houses have stucco walls, and one or two have wooden clapboards. All the roofs are tiled and steeply pitched, a matter of style rather than necessity. The vast majority of houses were built without chimneys – it took me a while to spot that – though one or two have had shiny metal chimneys added for wood-burning stoves. You can sometimes smell the smoke as you walk past. There are good hedges, good fences and good brick garden walls, which may well make for good neighbours.

But here's a thing: as far as I can ascertain, no two houses are quite the same. I've looked hard, and haven't found an exactly matching pair. Partly this may be because if you can get in early enough on a new-build, you can choose certain options to suit your own preference, but it seems to me that the developers of Lawford Dale deliberately included as many variations as possible within a basic design. Window arrangements, porches, styles of front door, guaranteed scope for a degree of difference, if not strictly speaking originality. My own house for instance has bricks of a colour unlike any other nearby. The house is detached whereas all the other chalet-styles are either semi-detached or part of a short terrace. My next door neighbour's house has the same footprint as mine, but the arrangement of her rooms is spun ninety degrees to mine.

Some houses are built with a single garage, some with a double, and – I found this hard to believe when I first saw it, there's at least one semi-detached house that has a detached double garage. Some have no garage at all, but usually there's some hard standing at the side of the house or in a corner of the garden, and sometimes a few houses are clustered together around a broad, shared driveway. This reduces the amount of garden, which no doubt suits some people, and saves them the trouble of gardening. But it also involves a serious loss of privacy. You're constantly driving your car past somebody else's front door, and other people are constantly driving past yours. You know their comings and goings and they know yours. It wouldn't suit some people at all; me for instance.

In fact I'd noticed that even when people had garages, very few were used to keep cars in. The majority of cars sat on driveways when they weren't out being driven. This didn't surprise me all that much. I know that a lot of people use their garages as workshops or for storage, and leaving your car outside wasn't much of a security issue. Lawford Dale did not, and still doesn't, seem to be a centre of rampant car theft.

My own house has a single garage and a short, unshared, driveway, though I didn't have a car when I first arrived. Since I'd been driving in the United States, on the 'wrong' side of the road for fifteen years and always in an automatic, I was a little nervous about driving in England, and so I tested the road by borrowing a car for a few days. It was a small, silver, characterless hatchback, as unremarkable and as suburban as any of my neighbours' vehicles. And I thought, to be on the safe side, since it wasn't mine, I'd keep it in my garage. It was a struggle to get it in there. The driveway met the garage door at a peculiar angle and there was a curving wall of the neighbour's garden on one side of the drive. I did manage to get the car into the garage, but then, it was a further struggle to open the car door. When the time came to get the car out again, things were even harder.

My neighbour had seen my difficulties and was kind enough not to question my driving skills, but I did ask her what kind of car the previous owner of my house had driven. She couldn't remember the make or model, but knew it was just an ordinary hatchback. 'Mind you,' she said, 'he always kept it on the drive, he never put it in the garage.' I already knew that she didn't garage her own car either. 'Oh, the garages around here,' she said, 'they're all ridiculously small. They built them that way because they knew they could charge more for a property if it had a garage, but you can hardly get a car into any of them. Mine's even worse than yours. I have to turn in my wing mirrors before I even try, so I don't bother.' When I got a car of my own, I never garaged it either.

There are also what struck me, when I first moved here, as a staggering number of huts and sheds, averaging at least one per household, probably more. My own house came with two sheds, one a surprisingly spacious lean-to which I use for storing tools, the other a positively huge, nicely fitted-out workshop, far in excess of any requirements I can ever imagine having.

I happened to know that the first chapter of Gaston Bachelard's *The Poetics of Space* is titled 'The House, from Cellar to Garret. The Significance of the Hut', and I thought he might have something relevant to say about huts and sheds, but it turns out that the kind of hut he has in mind really doesn't have much in common with any of the ones here. He's primarily concerned with the hermit's hut 'What a subject for an engraving! ... The hermit's hut is a theme which needs no variations, for at the simplest mention of it, "phenomenal reverberation" obliterates all mediocre resonances.' Well, only up to a point Gaston. I found something far more to my taste in Ed Dorn's *Gunslinger*. The horse is speaking:

> 'Here we are in the sheds
> and huts of the suburbs. There are
> some rigid types in here.
> It's kinda poignant ...'

Well yes, it is.

The cars belonging to residents here tend to be shiny, newish, smallish, ordinary: there are one or two sporty little numbers around, a few SUVs, Beamers and Mercs, but I've yet to see an old classic, or even an old banger. I've yet to see an *interesting* car. There are also, and at one time this surprised me, though I've now come to recognise it as a feature of much of suburbia, a certain number of camper vans and caravans parked in people's driveways, again mostly new and shiny. Part of the suburban idyll appears to involve the ability to travel away from home while still taking quite a few elements of your suburban life with you.

There's usually evidence of building work going on, lots of 'home improvement' – skips, double glazing being fitted or replaced, guttering being upgraded, rooftop solar panels being installed, extensions and conservatories being added. Although we're often told how conformist suburbia is, I constantly see people doing things differently from their neighbours, not wildly different, not inconceivably different, but just enough to assert their individuality, be it a new garage door, or some *faux* leaded windows.

John Ruskin had something to say about this: 'I would have, then, our ordinary dwelling-houses built to last, and built to be lovely; as rich and full of pleasantness as may be, within and without … with such differences as might suit and express each man's character and occupation, and partly his history.' I think about this a lot. Home improvement may not strictly speaking be a means of self-expression, but it's definitely a way of getting a place that suits you, as well as a way of making sure that your house isn't exactly like all the others in the street.

Is this a vulgar way of showing how much money you've got? A way of getting ahead of the Joneses? Well, no doubt some of it is. Those solar panels on the roofs, for instance, are they just virtue-signalling? Still, in the majority of cases, home improvement is also a way of increasing the value of the house, making it more desirable when you come to sell up and move on. But this isn't always straightforward. Sometimes you see people having massive amounts of work done on their house, spending a small fortune on projects that you think are scarcely going to increase the value at all, building a whole new 'wing' onto the back that takes up more than half the garden, making the house quite ugly in the process. But maybe this is narrow and penny-pinching of me to think only of resale value; worse, perhaps it's thoroughly *suburban* of me. And then there are other times when it seems perfectly admirable for people to say, 'Damn the expense, damn the resale value, I'm going to have my home exactly the way I want it.'

We all want a home that suits us, but that's not the same as having a house that expresses all our innermost quirks and desires. Does my house express who I am? Well, I prefer to think not, but I may be deceiving myself. I like to think it's a plain ordinary house that doesn't give too much away, but I expect the neighbours know more about me than I think they do. They've seen the furniture I've had delivered, they can see the mask of Mahakala attached to the garden shed, they may be able to peer through the windows and see the crammed bookcases, they may pass by and hear the music of Thurston Moore or Acid Mothers Temple being played at high volume. It's OK, the house is detached: I'm not bothering anybody.

I walk around the neighbourhood all the time, and I do see some other walkers, but not many. There are people walking with their kids, pushing prams, old couples going out together, overdressed whatever the weather. Depending on the time of day, there are men, it always seems to be men, walking to or from the station. They're going to or from jobs which may be in London or Colchester or Ipswich or Harwich. I imagine that these men would once have been wearing suits and carrying briefcases. These days they tend to wear chinos and have a rucksack on their back. I can't swear that they're any more contented or relaxed than their suited predecessors, but they're trying to look that way.

I see people walking their dogs: small bouncy, yappy things in the main, although I've seen one man walking a couple of retired greyhounds that look as though they could still outrun any of us. There are also a number of roaming cats. Some of them are skittish, though not all of them; there's one that sometimes comes running out to be petted. They come in various shades, and there used to be one I was particularly fond of that had a flash of dark fur coming down over one eye that made him look like Hitler.

In fact you could argue that the cats and dogs of the neighbourhood are a good deal more diverse than the people. No point pretending that this suburb is a melting pot of races and religions, although it's not by any means all white. There are certainly minorities living here but they're members of a smaller group than in any urban centre. This is hardly news.

Class-wise again, it's not fabulously diverse. One of my neighbours is a taxi driver, one's a schoolteacher, one's a landscape gardener, one's a recently retired university administrator. I'd say, if pressed, that they vary between the middle class and the upper working class, certainly there's nobody in these parts who seems upper class, though I accept that these are all dodgy terms. Many of my neighbours are former Londoners. They, or in some cases their parents, lived in the East End and they've gradually moved further east, first to places like Romford or Basildon, and then to Lawford. When they ask where I'm from, and they do, I say, 'From all over the place, but most recently London.' It seems easiest to say that I'm part of the great London/Essex diaspora than to say I've arrived after fifteen years in California.

The politics in these parts are largely Conservative. There's an active Labour presence, with members who sometimes hand out leaflets at the Farmers' Market at weekends, although evidently to no great effect. At the last election I didn't see any poster for any party in the window of any house in the neighbourhood. I didn't even receive an electoral leaflet from the Conservatives, which I took to be an indication that they were sure of victory without the likes of me, and they were right.

We did have one fringe candidate who, in his leaflet, defined himself as a Christian Independent: God was apparently not keen on Europe. Having been a police officer and a street warden, the candidate wrote, 'I have immersed myself in every aspect of the suburban human condition.' I wish I'd come up with that term. He received 0.5% of the vote.

Regardless of whom they vote for, the neighbours I've met seem genuinely decent. When I moved into the house, the high wall between me and the garden to the left was covered with a thick layer of miscellaneous growth that protruded a good few feet from the wall and ascended above head height. Most of what I could see was ivy but I knew there was some kind of small, spiky tree growing in there, supporting the whole thing. The first week I lived here it rained continuously for over seventy-two hours and on the morning of the third day, as I was eating breakfast and gazing out of the back window, I watched as the tree holding up the ivy very slowly pitched forward away from the wall, and moved through a full ninety degrees all the way to the ground, bringing with it most of the greenery, as well as a trellis which I hadn't even known was in there, along with chunks of moss and creeper, and several birds' nests.

Fortunately the garden wall was solid and stayed where it was but once the tree was down, half of my garden was covered in dense and deracinated foliage. I didn't know what to do, so I did nothing at first. In the afternoon of that day, one of my neighbours, who I hadn't met till then, came to my back gate and peered into the garden. I was in the house, still unpacking, and I went out to see what she wanted. She was relieved to see me, she said, and asked me if was all right. She'd been looking out of her bedroom window, seen the mighty pile of greenery on my lawn, and feared that I might be under it. I assured her that I was fine, and explained what had happened, and I did think, though I didn't say, that if I'd really been pinned down under that pile for all those hours, I might well have been beyond help.

Is there a sense of community here? I wouldn't say so, and I imagine people prefer it that way. Yes, occasionally we moan to each other about the fecklessness and incompetence of the council, but we don't want to have *meetings* about it.

And what do my neighbours get up to behind the curtains and the locked doors? I have absolutely no idea. Do they have dark urges and secret lives? Well, I'm sure some of them do because that's what people are like: these things are everywhere, as much in suburbia as anywhere else. The difference, I think, is that in suburbia people are pretty good at keeping secrets. You don't look at an unassuming semi-detached house and immediately think, ah yes, a couple of enthusiasts for dogging and opioids live here: and that's a good thing, that's the way they, and the rest of us, prefer it. The suburban virtue of keeping yourself to yourself has enormous advantages, for everyone.

If we can debate the extent to which a house is a medium of self-expression, people's front gardens inevitably say something about them whether they want them to or not. A garden may simply be saying, 'The people who live here have absolutely no interest in gardening,' or it may say, 'The people who live here are only prepared to do the absolute minimum,' but generally it says more than that.

To be fair, few of the local gardens are wildly extravagant or eccentric. A number face the world with a neat blankness, a rectangle of lawn, a path, some shrubs, maybe a few potted plants. A greater number are well tended but unspectacular, so it's the small manifestations of individuality and creativity that count, and that really stand out. Statuary, for want of a better word, is the prime means of making a statement. So, there's a garden nearby decorated with a pair of stone swans, another where the Loch Ness Monster is coming up out of the lawn. There are stone rabbits and cats, lions, meerkats, a pig in dungarees, a Buddha. These are no doubt store-bought, and the means of expression has been only one of selection and purchase, but there is one garden that has seven blocks of stone, henges perhaps, each about two feet tall, arranged not quite randomly in the grass. Its inscrutability is its appeal, and although I walk past it all the time, I've yet to see the inhabitant of the house.

And there's one garden that absolutely stands out because it's so different from all the others, and so utterly unlike the received idea of what any suburban garden should be. It looks like it belongs in Torquay, or possibly Cannes. It has palm trees that actually bear dates, a couple of benches, expanses of white gravel, giant terracotta Ali Baba-style pots, and the centerpiece is an olive tree as big as any I've ever seen in England.

I'm not convinced that the inhabitants of Lawford Dale are passionate environmentalists, but there's evidence of a lot of recycling going on: bins sitting by front doors and in front gardens. You don't need to be some hardcore aesthete to find these things an eyesore. You also wonder whether flooding the neighbourhood with plastic containers in order to collect other plastic containers is any advantage in the long run. It would be nice to think somebody had done a calculation about this.

The neighbourhood is 'quiet', of course, but there are the sounds of cars, and some tradesmen's vans, and increasing numbers of vehicles delivering all the things that get ordered online. There are one or two kids who come by on motorbikes and scooters, with throaty or damaged exhausts. If it's a weekend in summer you'll hear the sounds of people mowing their lawns, and also people vacuuming the interior of their cars. I wasn't expecting that. I knew about car washing of course but the vacuuming came as a surprise. I have certainly washed cars and shaken out the rubber floor mats, but I've never vacuumed the interior of one.

Sometimes there's music coming out of open windows, but even in the summer that's rare, and there's somebody nearby who practises the drums, not all that well, and never for very long, mostly on weekday afternoons. There are the sounds of birds, pigeons primarily though there are gulls and crows and magpies and lots of little chirping things. There are the yappy dogs I mentioned.

Trains regularly rattle and reverberate in the distance, mostly passenger trains though there are also louder goods trains, but I never find that noise intrusive. It always sounds reassuring, and sometimes it sounds like a sign or a safety valve, evidence of an escape route. This suburb of mine is easy to get to and easy to get away from: London is just an hour away, and that's important to me, that's where a substantial part of my life still takes place. I am profoundly attached to, and in many ways dependent on, the big city, and that's true of many suburbanites.

Is life dull here? Is it too uneventful? Well yes and no. I was a little disappointed by my first Halloween here. I thought lots of houses would be draped with skeletons, skulls, cobwebs, ghostly apparitions in the form of old bed sheets, but all I saw were a few drooping pumpkins. Therefore I wasn't expecting too much at Christmas, and was surprised by the amount of work people put into festooning their houses and gardens with lights. My next door neighbour, the one on the other side from the lady who was concerned about my demise under the ivy, really went to town – he does every year – animated reindeer, snowmen, Santa Clauses, pulsing snowflakes.

But the truth is, I don't expect these suburban streets to provide me with entertainment and stimulation. And I like to think there's something Zen about living here. I'm not a Zen disciple and I'm certainly not a Buddhist – that whole reincarnation business doesn't sit well with me – but as I walk around the neighbourhood it's the small things, the minor variations, the specific and muted signs of humanity and personality that make life worth living. The man up the street is laying a new patio. The lady on the corner is having a good year with her grapevine. And I think this is some version of Zen enlightenment. You look at an unexpected olive tree and you become enlightened, you look at a stone swan and you become enlightened, you look at a new piece of guttering, ditto. It is also some part, an important part, of being a writer: noticing things and setting them down.

So for now I'm here in the suburbs, and have been for a while, making the best of it, and the fact is, I do *like* it here. I *like* the suburbs. There, I said it. There are things to see, things to enjoy, things to think about, although I will also confess that sometimes it seems to me that the real cause of my being here, the main reason I came to live here, was because I thought there might be a book in it.

2

Definers, Haters and Others

You know what a suburb is. I know what a suburb is. Possibly we'd be in complete agreement, possibly not, but whatever we agreed upon, we could find people who would disagree strongly about the defining features of a suburb in terms of location, its relation to a city or town, its building types, whether it's defined by who does and doesn't live there, whether it's to do with class, race, social, political or gender norms, about what it is and what it isn't, about what it does and doesn't do.

The *Oxford English Dictionary* is only partially helpful, offering this basic definition of a suburb, 'The country lying immediately outside a town or city; more particularly, those residential parts belonging to a town or city that lie immediately outside and adjacent to its walls or boundaries.'

It's not wrong exactly, but that word 'country' (in the sense of 'countryside') is the big problem, because the suburbs seem to be no part of the countryside, in fact they seem to stand in some fundamental opposition to it. Some would say suburbs are the very things that *ruin* the country by being dropped into what was once open fields, thereby destroying the natural environment.

Another problem with that definition is the extent to which so many suburbs are within city boundaries. Yes, we can imagine an early walled city with gates and fortifications, so that the suburbs were what grew up outside and around it, but when there are no walls, and in cities where boundaries regularly change and generally extend outwards, suburbs are often *within* the city.

The problem goes back to the Latin origin of the word. It comes from *suburbium* (plural *suburbia*), the combination of *urbs* meaning city, and *sub* meaning below, and most usually referring to the city of Rome. Since ancient Rome was built on seven hills, there was plenty of scope for people to live in the lower reaches. So this kind of suburb is below the city both physically and in terms of status: the latter notion being still with us, though there are quite a few suburbs that are physically *above* the city; two that I know are Clifton in Bristol, and Broomhill in Sheffield. Both are considered rather superior and desirable suburbs, precisely because they were built on the heights above the mess and commerce of the city.

The *OED* cites John Wycliffe's translation of the Bible, *circa* 1380, where it generally means the agricultural land surrounding a city, so we're back to the 'country' again, and there's a reference to 'the suburbs of Gomorrah', fields which produce very sour grapes.

The King James Bible keeps the word suburb in Leviticus, and uses it extensively throughout the text, but in Deuteronomy it has become fields. Perhaps the 'suburbs of Gomorrah' just sounded a little bit too enticing.

Chaucer uses 'suburbes' in the Canon Yeoman's Prologue and Tale, written some time towards the end of the fourteenth century. Shakespeare uses 'suburbs' eight times in his works, most evocatively in *Julius Caesar*, (1599), when Portia says to Brutus,

> Dwell I but in the suburbs
> Of your good pleasure? If it be no more,
> Portia is Brutus' harlot, not his wife.

We can see that even if the suburbs are currently thought to represent respectability and a quiet if boring life, it was by no means always that way. At one time suburbs were considered to be places of vice and decadence. Thomas Nashe in *Christ's Tears Over Jerusalem* (1593) writes, 'London, what are thy Suburbes but licenced Stewes?'

History brings up some strange, wonderful and now unused forms of the word: suburbial (1602), suburbian (1606), suburbican (1659), suburbicarial (1688). The nineteenth century brought us more familiar forms, though by no means all of them in common use today: suburbanism, suburbanites, suburbanity. In 1825 C.M. Westmacott, in his book *The English Spy*, describes a town-and-gown battle in Oxford which included the 'scum of the suburbians'.

The twentieth century brought us suburbandom, suburbanise and suburbanisation, along with a couple of 'special collocations' – suburban neurosis, 1938, and suburban sprawl, 1949. I can't decide whether it's significant or not that the neurosis preceded the sprawl.

The word suburbia first appeared as part of a book title, *A Street in Suburbia,* a collection of humorous short stories published by Edwin W. Pugh in 1895: not as humorous as all that, trust me, I've read it so that you don't have to.

It seems that ever since the word suburb has been current there have been metaphorical usages. Thomas Nashe, again, speaks of 'the wayward suburbes of my narration', De Quincey writes of 'the immediate suburbs of midsummer', Longfellow tells us, 'This Mortal breath is but a suburb of the life elysian.'

It seems odd, and I stand to be corrected, but as far as I can see there's no absolutely convincing synonym for suburb. We can talk about commuter belts, outskirts, fringes, estates, sub-divisions, developments, but none of them has quite the same meanings and connotations as that apparently simple word, 'suburb', which is perhaps to say that it's not such a simple word after all.

Sometimes people use the word suburb to mean simply neighbourhood, which I think misses the point. The online world is full of articles and listicles telling you which are the best suburbs to live in in Sydney, Tokyo, Mexico City or Mumbai. The answers, according to at least one online source, are respec-tively Tumbi Umbi, Azabu, Coyoacán and Bandra West known as 'the Queen of Suburbs'. But this can be very misleading, if not downright meaningless. Similar articles will tell you that the best suburb in Rio de Janeiro, for example, is Copacabana, which conforms to nobody's idea of a suburb. These people just seem to have no idea what a suburb really is.

It isn't only lexicographers who try to define 'suburb'. A surprising number of academics of various disciplines – sociology, urban studies, history, literary criticism, among them – are doing the same in order to clarify what it is they're studying. The best overview I've found is an article by Ann Forsyth, titled simply 'Defining Suburbs', which appeared in 'The Journal of Planning Literature', in 2013.

Forysth recounts the struggle of trying to define a suburb by its salient features, the obvious ones: suburbs are outside of a town or city but they belong to it, they're primarily middle class, low-density, low-rise, with chiefly single-family dwellings, which means naturally that the number of nuclear families will be high. The politics will be conservative at least with a small c, the inhabitants will aim to be respectable (whatever *that* means), the architecture will be unspectacular, and at least in countries with predominantly white populations (Britain, the United States, Australia where most of Forsyth's studies come from) there will be comparatively few non-white residents.

At first glance this seems fair enough but even she realizes that it soon starts to unravel. She points out that an area inside a city may be quite 'suburban' in design or look or feel (although of course that only leads us back to the question of what we mean by suburban in this context), some early suburbs were more densely populated than the centres of cities, and she quotes Jon C. Teaford's book *The American Suburbs: The Basics* (2007) in which the author writes,

> Suburbs include some of the nation's most densely popu-
> lated communities as well as areas zoned to accommodate
> more horses than human beings. Suburbia reflects the
> ethnic diversity of America more accurately than the
> central cities, providing homes for Hispanics, Asians,
> and Blacks as well as non-Hispanic whites. It comprises
> slums as well as mansions, main streets as well as malls,
> skyscrapers as well as schools. Some suburbs are particu-
> larly gay-friendly; others are planned for senior citizens.
> Some are known for their fine schools; others are examples
> of educational failure.

He is, of course, talking about American suburbs, but apart from the mention of horses I think most of that can be applied to Britain.

Forsyth lists varying *types* of suburb, some of which I'd never previously encountered, either in print or in the field:

technoburbs, ethnoburbs, and she mentions, though doesn't define, something called postsuburbia.

One source she doesn't cite is *The Anglo-American Suburb* (1981) by Robert A.M. Stern and John Massengale, which again makes distinctions between different kinds of suburb. These include railroad suburbs, industrial villages, resort suburbs, streetcar, subway and automobile suburbs, though there's no mention here of garden suburbs, which seems surprising.

Another crucial source, and a favourite of mine, which Forsyth does mention, is Delores Hayden's marvellous *A Field Guide to Sprawl* (2004), with aerial photographs by Jim Wark. It's a serious book but it's also lots of fun. It largely consists of what the author calls 'an illustrated vocabulary of sprawl'. Not all of these terms refer directly to our usual idea of the suburbs though many do, including boomburb, edge nodes, mall glot, privatopia, leapfrog development and zoomburb. Perhaps, above all, this shows that in the current cultural climate, the word suburb can no longer stand alone, but always needs a qualifier. This is also to say that despite their reputation for uniformity and homogeneity, not all suburbs are equal, nor intended to be.

Forsyth points out that 'Many definitions of suburbs are really catalogs of their ills,' and so we come to the haters.

Many people are *proud* to hate the suburbs. The hating can be done on personal or social or political or environmental or aesthetic grounds. No doubt on other grounds too, though truly novel and original reasons for hating the suburbs are hard to come by. As things stand, chances are, whatever your reasons, you won't be alone in your hatred, you'll be part of a tradition.

A gloriously immoderate early denunciation can be found in *The Suburbans* (1905) by T.W.H. Crosland, who was a friend of Alfred Douglas after the Oscar Wilde trial. Crosland's views on the suburbs are pretty straightforward. He hates them. He writes, 'Whatever, in short, strikes the superior mind as being deficient in completeness, excellence and distinction may with absolute safety be called suburban'.

The book goes on for two hundred pages (it seems longer), dismissing all the people and the qualities of suburbia. 'Sound people insist upon their tradesmen waiting upon them, the stupid and barbarian suburbans wait upon their tradesmen,' although I have to say that when I'm waiting in for an Amazon delivery this does seem to have some validity.

Crosland denounces architects, 'It is the architect who has made the ugly face of suburbia ugly beyond tolerance; it is the architect who has made it preposterous beyond preposterousness; it is the architect whose cheek ought to flame, and whose liver ought to wither at the sight of it all.'

And to be fair, some architects are at least as anti-suburb as Crosland. Le Corbusier was a prime mover behind *Congrés Internationaux d'Achitecture Moderne* (1933), which described suburbs as 'a kind of scum, churning against the walls of the city' and 'one of the greatest evils of the century'. This became part of the Athens Statement and eventually part of Le Corbusier's *La Ville Radieuse*. It seems to us now that 1933 was a very bad year to be pontificating about suburbs as the century's 'greatest evils'.

However, Richard Rogers, an architect of a considerably later generation, wouldn't have found much to disagree with in Le Corbusier's statement. He wrote, 'Suburban sprawl leads to social atomisation and fragmentation and is environmentally disastrous, as carbon-intensive car journeys displace local shops and replace public transport.' That was in an article for the *Evening Standard* in 2013. He singled out Croydon as the worst of the worst.

Architectural commentators are inclined to pile on the agony. In *The City in History* (1961), Lewis Mumford berated suburbia as 'an asylum for the preservation of illusion', asserting that that suburban residents were not only withdrawing from the city, they were shrinking from civic responsibility in general. I think he may have a point here, although obviously not all city dwellers take their civic responsibilities very seriously either.

James Howard Kunstler, a man who (if his website is to be believed) has made a career out of denouncing the suburbs in TED talks and lectures at Yale, Cornell, MIT and other institutions, writes in *The Geography of Nowhere: the Rise and Decline of America's Man-Made Landscape* (1993), 'I like to call it the "national automobile slum". You can call it suburban sprawl. I think it's appropriate to call it the greatest misallocation of resources in the history of the world.'

But, of course, you don't have to be a professional architect or architectural commentator to hate the suburbs. 'Slums may well be breeding grounds of crime, but middle-class suburbs are incubators of apathy and delirium.' That's Cyril Connolly, writing as Palinurus, in *The Unquiet Grave* (1944), in a section titled 'Ecce Gubernator'. I like that he seems to be raising a distinction between middle-class suburbs and others. Working class suburbs? Yes, I think they exist. Upper-class suburbs? I'm not so sure. Suburbs can certainly be very expensive, though I don't think they can be aristocratic.

Suburbia for Beryl Gilroy, a member of the Windrush Generation, a poet, novelist, educational theorist and one of Britain's first Black headteachers, 'is a sort of twilight country, indeterminate between sleeping and waking, muted and barely alive'. That's from her memoir *Black Teacher* (1976). She taught in a school in West Hampstead, a place where I once lived in a tiny rented flat.

There's John Betjeman of course who invited friendly bombs to fall on Slough!' a troubling line to have written at any time but especially so in 1934. History caught up with him and ensured that his poetic, and no doubt rhetorical, wish to bomb Slough came true.

At least Betjeman's hatred of Slough in the poem is multi-faceted, and not the same old same old. He laments the lack of grazing room for cows. He hates men who talk about sport.

He hates mock-Tudor pubs, women who paint their nails, mortgages, labour-saving homes, air conditioning, the eating and thinking habits of the inhabitants, 'Tinned fruit, tinned meat, tinned milk, tinned beans, Tinned minds, tinned breath.'

Chances are that most of us hate one or two of those things he condemns, but it's hard to hate all of them. What's so terrible about labour-saving homes? Betjeman was in his early thirties when he wrote the poem, so we can't put it down to youthful anarchism, and according to his daughter Candida Lycett Green he regretted ever having written those words. Poets, like anyone else, are allowed to change their minds.

An unlikely fellow traveller for Betjeman is William Upski Wimsatt, author of a book titled *Bomb the Suburbs* (1994), though the contents aren't quite as angry as that title sounds. And since Wimsatt was writing about American hiphop culture and street art, which to some degree he was a part of (Upski was his graffiti tagging name), the title is a kind of pun: the bombing refers to tagging as much as to real-world explosions.

He writes,

> I say bomb the suburbs because the suburbs have been bombing us for at least the last forty years. They have waged an economic, political, and cultural war on life in the city. The city has responded by declaring war on itself. *Bomb the Suburbs* is a message to people who live in the city. It is a call to change your strategy. Stop bombing the city. Stop bombing the ghetto. Stop fucking up your own neighborhoods and taking your frustrations out on those around you.

That sounds fair enough to me.

Wimsatt changed his mind too. In 2010 he published another book, *Please Don't Bomb the Suburbs*, subtitled 'A Midterm Report on My Generation and the Future of Our Super Movement',

When Wimsatt was publicising the book he was inevitably asked why he no longer wanted to bomb the suburbs. Here's the reply he gave to Lauri Apple in an interview for the *Chicago Reader* website,

> I wrote *Bomb the Suburbs* before the Oklahoma City bombing, and before September 11. It was a cute thing back then, when it was just referring to graffiti.
>
> Also, the suburbs aren't what they used to be! And cities aren't what they used to be. In the last sixteen years, since *Suburbs* came out, the suburbs have gotten a lot more diverse, and with a lot more poor people.

The implication here is that it's OK to approve of suburbia if you approve of the people who live there.

Not all the people cited above ever lived in the suburbs, which obviously doesn't mean that they're not entitled to an opinion, it's just that those opinions are likely to be of the broad, distant, lofty, wrong-end-of-the-telescope variety. A different kind of hatred comes from people who actually live or have lived in the suburbs. The novelist Hari Kunzru: 'Suburbia is all about private ownership and not having to share, and it leads to a paranoid, defensive mindset. I know this, having grown up in Essex.' That's Essex between London's North Circular Road and the M25 (by Junction 26 in Kunzru's own account). At a 2015 event named Doughnut: The Outer London Festival, Will Self described the suburbs as the 'spatialisation of patriarchy' – he was partly brought up in Hampstead Garden Suburb.

Tracy Thorne of the band Everything But The Girl, wrote a volume of memoirs (her second) titled *Another Planet: A Teenager in Suburbia* (2018), about growing up in Brookmans Park, a place just sixteen miles north of London. Naturally she argued with her parents as she grew up, and writes,

I told them I wanted to marry a poet and live in London. I wanted to get out. I couldn't understand why they had ever moved here in the first place. Why would anyone want to? Who would choose suburbia? It's for squares, for drones, worst of all, for PARENTS, who love it for the quality of life it offers. Young people don't care about such things as comfort and cleanliness – they want culture, and nightlife, and energy. There are no clubs or pavement cafés in suburbia. You can't explore it at night, as – say – Dickens walked the streets of London. Who walks around suburbia at night? You can't be a suburban *flâneur*.

Well, trust me you can be, and personally I am, but I take her general point. She concludes, 'No wonder we looked at suburbia and wanted to burn it down.' But of course she didn't burn it down. She moved to Hampstead, not to live with a poet exactly, but with Ben Watt, the other half of Everything But The Girl. I don't think this is hypocrisy, but I do think it indicates that beliefs we have as teenagers may not last a whole lifetime.

The relationship between the suburbs and popular music is a complex one. Of the making of songs about suburbia, there is, apparently, no end. A very small, though not quite random, sample includes the Pet Shop Boys' 'Suburbia', Manfred Mann's 'Semi-Detached, Suburban Mr. James' (originally Jones), 'Suburban Relapse' by Siouxsie and the Banshees – Siouxsie Sioux, née Susan Ballion, grew up in Chislehurst, though was considered part of the Bromley Contingent. There's also David Bowie's 'Buddha of Suburbia', which was the title song for the TV adaptation of the Hanif Kureishi novel, the video for which was filmed in St Matthew's Drive, Bickley. There's Pulp's 'Stylorock (Nites of Suburbia)' and the Bonzo Dog Band's 'My Pink Half of the Drainpipe.'

These songs describe suburbia variously as a place where we run with the dogs, where we hang out the washing as our life slips away, where we slide into recurrent spousal abuse (that's the suburban relapse of the Siouxsie Sioux song), where we live in lies by the railway line, where we sprout black hair beneath Bry-Nylon underwear, and where, we might be baffled by 'cabbages and rhinoceroses in the kitchen [and] incessant quotations from *Now We Are Six* through the mouthpiece of Lord Snooty's giant poisoned electric head'.

We could add plenty of other songs too: Ray Charles's 'I'm Gonna Move to the Outskirts of Town', a not especially 'woke' song about moving to the edge of town where the singer's woman will have fewer opportunities for adultery, Rush's 'Subdivision', Richard E. Kirk's 'The Truck Bombers of Suburbia' and The Cribs 'Screaming in Suburbia'. Arcade Fire made a whole album about the suburbs, titled *The Suburbs,* which inspired Spike Lee to make a thirty-minute movie. The opening lyric from the title song was: 'In the suburbs I learned to drive/And you told me I'd never survive,' but, you know, somehow they did.

In my teenage years in Sheffield there was a local combo called The Spaced Band who had a song titled 'Welcome to Suburbia'. Memory being what it is, I recall the opening line clearly, 'I just got back from inner space, it's overcrowded there.' I think the song was about a man who's taken a bad acid trip and afterwards decides to live the rest of his life quietly in the suburbs. All these songs have their appeal and their fans. I was thrilled to listen again, for the first time in a long time, to Frank Zappa's 'It Can't Happen Here', a song with a good few layers of irony, that asserts that 'it' (i.e. freaking out) can happen anywhere, though nobody can believe it will happen where they live.

Who could imagine
Who could imagine

That they would freak out in the suburbs
I remember (tu-tu)
I remember (tu-tu)
I remember (tu-tu)
They had a swimming pool.

And I admit I'd forgotten the line in the Doors' 'L.A. Woman',

L.A. woman Sunday afternoon
Drive through your suburbs
Into your blues, into your blues, yeah.

And let's definitely not forget the line about 'blue suburban skies' in the Beatles' 'Penny Lane'.

OK, not all these songs are entirely, or only, *about* the suburbs, but they're certainly all songs *informed* by the suburbs. But for me no song gets it quite as right as The Members' 1979 hit single 'The Sound of the Suburbs', written by the band's guitarist Jean-Marie Carroll, and singer Nick Lightowlers (aka Nicky Tesco), two lads from Camberley, in the Heathrow flight path and close to Broadmoor. The song is sometimes described as a punk anthem, but The Members weren't really punk, or not very convincingly so. They were post-punk at best. The song feels like a pastiche of punk, in parts even a parody.

It starts out with some familiar suburban images of dad washing the car and mum cooking Sunday dinner,

And Johnny's upstairs in his bedroom sitting in the dark
Annoying the neighbours with his punk rock electric guitar.

So far, so unsurprising, but later there's the gorgeous couplet,

Youth club group used to wanna be free,
now they want ANARCHY!

which seems to mock Johnny Rotten wannabees just as much as it mocks Richie Havens wannabees: part-time punks as well as weekend hippies, though I suspect that most suburban youth club groups never really knew *what* they wanted.

And in at least one online version of the lyrics there's a final verse (which I've never heard in any of the versions of the song I've listened to) that's strangely touching and, I think, sincere,

> Out there in the wilderness
> There's a boy playing the guitar
> He's dreaming of writing a song
> That will take him far far far away from there.

The Members' song shares some DNA with 'Pleasant Valley Sunday', written by Jerry Goffin and Carole King, and a hit for the Monkees. The opening lines are,

> The local rock group down the street
> Is trying hard to learn their song

It sounds as though a few solitary suburban Johnnies have found band mates to play with, which may well be better than sitting alone in a bedroom in the dark. For a long time I assumed the song was about the San Gabriel Valley, northwest of Los Angeles, but in fact it's about New Jersey. Goffin and King, a married couple at the time, had (for inscrutable reasons) moved from Brooklyn to West Orange, a suburb of Newark where there was a street named Pleasant Valley Way. Mark Twain said, 'There's something nice about Newark. I think it's the suburbs,' though Goffin and King apparently felt differently.

Now, you might think that since Goffin and King had willingly chosen to live in the suburbs of Newark they would have an interesting or surprising or paradoxical take on things, but no, their song contains some weary, standard-issue complaints about the materialism and conformity of suburbia,

> Creature comfort goals, they only numb my soul
> And make it hard for me to see.

'Pleasant Valley Sunday' (which King in recent times has sung with a huge, happy smile on her face, and with James Taylor providing cheery background harmonies) in turn seems to share DNA with 'Little Boxes', a song written in 1962 by Malvina Reynolds, and a hit for Pete Seeger the next year. It was apparently inspired by the large quantity of suburban housing being built around Daly City, in California, where Reynolds was living at the time, which suggests the song was born of NIMBYISM as much as anti-suburban, anti-capitalist rhetoric. One verse runs,

> And the people in the houses
> All went to the university
> Where they were put in boxes
> And they came out all the same
> And there's doctors and lawyers
> And business executives
> And they're all made out of ticky tacky
> And they all look just the same.

Sneering at lawyers and business executives again seems standard practice, although sneering at doctors, even if they live in suburbia, seems a bit uncharitable to me.

This tendency for inhabitants of the pop and rock world to curl their lips at those less bohemian, less hip and less arty than themselves is common enough, but like it or not, suburbia is where so much popular music comes from. Mick Jagger and Keith Richards came from respectively the right and wrong suburban ends of Dartford, Kate Bush lived in

Bexleyheath – full disclosure, in the house right next to my former, late grandmother-in-law. Both Sterling Morrison and Mo Tucker came from Levittown on Long Island. John Cage grew up in an Arts and Crafts-style bungalow in Eagle Rock, Los Angeles.

Paul Weller is a son of Woking who lived in Stanley Road, which is also the title of a surprisingly warm and benign song from 1995 about growing up there; surprising largely because fifteen years earlier Weller had written 'A Town Called Malice' also about Woking.

In his collected lyrics Weller writes about that earlier song, 'There was a phony pretence that we could suddenly all become middle class because we were allowed to buy our own homes, get a mortgage and be in debt for the rest of our lives.' No, Paul, that's really not how mortgages work. The title of those collected lyrics is *Suburban 100*.

Incidentally, Weller's Stanley Road abuts Maybury Road, where H.G. Wells lived while writing *The War of the Worlds*,

> The detachment of the plaster had left a vertical slit open in the debris, and by raising myself cautiously across a beam I was able to see out of this gap into what had been overnight a quiet suburban roadway. Vast, indeed, was the change that we beheld.

It's true enough that not many professional pop and rock musicians find themselves living in deepest suburbia. The successful ones buy country mansions and collect art and classic cars; the unsuccessful ones live in the cheapest parts of town, and struggle to keep their tour van running. Both, I suppose, are free of the usual suburban pressures and worries, which is not to say that they don't have pressures and worries of a different kind. On the other hand, the suburbs are not at all lacking in men and women, more of the former than the latter of course, who can proudly boast, 'I used to be in a band, you know,' but who gave it up to do something more 'regular' which earns them the money to be able to live in suburbia.

I have friends in Los Angeles who helped me discover the Controllers, a punk band who made a fabulous single in 1977 titled 'Suburban Suicide', with the lyrics,

> City girls tell us lies
> They don't like suburban guys
> City girls from over the hill
> City girls love to kill

Those words contain something not widely acknowledged: that suburban kids aren't only angry with their parents, they're also angry with their hipper, more sophisticated, better-connected metropolitan contemporaries who dismiss them as mugs. However, the song does contain references to long drives on the freeways, which is rarely part of the British suburban experience. If you're young and British, and live in the suburbs, you tend to think that all your problems would be solved if only you could drive and had a car.

In the rap world there are few putdowns more damning than the term 'suburban rap', which stands in opposition to gangsta rap, and possibly every other kind of rap, and is a double-edged condemnation, both of rappers who make the kind of music enjoyed by kids in suburbia (mostly white, inevitably), but also of the rappers *from* the suburbs. This includes acts such as De La Soul (who came together in Amityville, Long Island), Chance the Rapper (from West Chatham, Chicago – his dad worked for the mayor and for Obama, his mother worked for the Illinois attorney general) and Childish Gambino (born on an airforce base, raised in Stone, Georgia as a Jehovah's Witness, got a degree in Dramatic Writing from NYU), all of whom strike me as rather good and sophisticated performers, but then I suppose I *would* think that. But again this is not straightforward. Kanye West, who is not generally thought of as suburban, was raised in the pretty comfortable Oak Lawn suburb of Chicago, by a mother who was a professor of English.

Some suburban rappers are white, which only makes everything worse. MC Lars, who's from Pebble Beach, California, and was educated at Stanford and Oxford, probably gets it coming and going, not least with his song 'Rap Girl',

> Suburban rap queen, I wrote this song for you
> Suburban rap queen, what's a MC to do
> Suburban rap queen, every Biggie needs a Kim
> Suburban rap queen, sometimes you lose sometimes you win

If you haven't heard it, trust me, it's worse than it might appear from the lyrics, though to be honest the real problem is not its suburbanity.

Finally, just in case you suspect there are no pro-suburb songs, and there surely aren't many, and none I suspect written in living memory, bear in mind 'The Suburb Song', words by Marion Scott, music by Harold E. Darke, published in 1912. It's actually the somewhat official song of Hampstead Garden Suburb but I'm sure it can have wider applications. The lyrics of the first verse run as follows:

> Come all who think that songs are good.
> A joyous song we'll sing
> And praise our Garden Suburb home
> Until the echoes ring.

Well, what kind of monster doesn't think songs are good?

It's perfectly possible to find people who don't hate suburbia, people who live there for instance, people who *love* living there

and who wouldn't want to live anywhere else. The problem is
that these people tend not to write academic papers or punk
anthems, and very few of them produce books. Some of them do
get interviewed and quoted from time to time, but when their
remarks appear in print or on screen, the chances are there'll be
some ironic or distancing framework around them.

Bill Owens's book of photographs, titled simply *Suburbia*,
is not immune to this tendency, but it's an enormously likeable
work, and although it, and Owens, sometimes seem amused
by the inhabitants of suburbia, it's not scathing or malicious.
It was first published in 1973, and in a revised edition in 1999,
and consists of photographs taken in Livermore in California,
where Owens lived at the time. Yes, great photographers can
live in suburbia. The pictures show lots of parties, people
gardening, people with their cars, playing with their kids,
a woman vacuuming the deepest shag carpet I've ever seen.
But the captions are as important as the images. These are
quotations from the people in the photographs, Owens's neighbours, and although these are generally positive statements,
depending on your point of view it's possible to find them
banal or absurd.

A couple spoon-feeding a baby who's been set on a kitchen
worktop are quoted as saying, 'We are really happy. Our kids
are healthy, we eat good food. And we have a really nice house.'
It's hard to find much fault with that, but a different photograph shows two men sitting behind a small bar in a domestic
living room. One of them says, 'My hobby is drinking. On the
weekends I enjoy getting together with my friends and boozing.'
Hard not to chuckle at that one.

Everyone in Livermore seems happy enough, though they're
not blinkered: a Chinese family complains about being unable
to find Chinese food in the area, a woman says she can't do her
housework knowing that babies are being killed in Vietnam.
And there's a man who says, 'I find a sense of freedom in the

suburbs … You assume the mask of suburbia for outward appearances and yet no one knows what you really do.'

A British photographer, Daniel Meadows, undertook a similar project in England, which became the book *Nattering in Paradise* (1988), though there are more words than pictures, with long transcribed interviews. Kathy Morgan, described as a 'newcomer from the Midlands', says, 'Yes, suburbia, is accessible to both the town and the countryside, it really is a midway point. Yes, here it's the land of opportunity.'

Inevitably, the English class system figures. Andrew, described as a 'journalist and lefty', says

> Most of the people round here tend to be money snobs. Archetypal outer-London suburbanites … There are a lot of very nice people, it's just that many of them are inner-London people and there's nobody more calculated to be a roaring Tory than someone of working- or lower-middle-class origins who comes from the more built-up inner-London districts.

Suburbanites are not guaranteed to feel respect for their fellow suburbanites.

Meadows's 'paradise' is set in a part of suburbia which he calls The Borough, and he doesn't specify more than that, but there are clues. One of the inhabitants says that Margaret and Dennis Thatcher lived 'round the corner at the Dormers, twenty years or more ago'. That pins it down as Farnborough. The Thatchers were sometime suburbanites, and apparently happy enough there. In 1979 Margaret was described as 'the sweetheart of the suburbs', by the *Newcastle Evening Chronicle*. However, the Thatchers' presence in the suburbs was intermittent. They moved to Farnborough when their rent in Chelsea got too high, and the Farnborough house came with one and a half acres of garden, so a very superior and expensive kind of suburb.

After Farnborough they moved to Westminster (not suburban), then to Lamberhurst (suburban enough – Dennis liked the golf club there), then back to Chelsea, then to the flat above Number 10. On the day Margaret Thatcher left office the couple moved to a five-bedroom mock-Gothic Barrett Home in Dulwich, but they didn't stay there long either before moving to a mansion in Belgravia. After the death of Dennis, Margaret ended her days living in the Ritz Hotel, which I think is not part of the suburban dream, though personally I like the sound of it.

We've seen how architects loathe, or are supposed to loathe, the suburbs, but one who didn't was Terry Farrell. I used to be a near neighbour of his (though he didn't know it) when I lived in London in Maida Vale, a suburb, kind of, which had been predominantly Jewish in the late nineteenth and early twentieth centuries, though by the time I arrived there it had a reputation as bedsitland, and by the time I left there were men in Islamic robes holding meetings in the basement of the corner shop.

As I explored the neighbourhood, I discovered that just occasionally, here and there, dotted among the mansion blocks and the big white stucco houses, it was possible to see a few unexpected semi-detached houses. And the most extraordinary of these was a curious and intriguing house in Ashworth Road, close to the Tube station and the Paddington Recreation Ground. I didn't take any photographs all the time I lived there, and now I wish I had, but I recall an essentially conventional-looking house that had been made wild and wonderful by the addition of some colourful, angular, and perhaps post-modern, architectural elements.

I eventually worked out that the house belonged to Terry Farrell, a name I barely knew at the time, though I, and the rest of London, soon got to know his name and quite a few of his buildings; Clifton Nurseries in Covent Garden, the Channel

Four building in Camden, with the giant egg cups on the roof, Charing Cross Station, and eventually the MI6 headquarters.

In due course I read Farrell's 2004 book, *Place: A Story of Modelmaking, Menageries and Paper Rounds*, in which he writes:

> I bought a semi-detached 1924 house in Ashworth Road, Maida Vale, which Sue and I moved to – and which became the family home for us and our children for more than 25 years. Friends told me I was 'very brave' because the house represented everything most architects had been told to rebel against. That was one of the reasons why it appealed to me. I was determined to show what could be done with a standard between-the-wars, semi-detached, speculative house whose very ordinariness would make it a place for living, growing and enjoying life without over intrusive 'architecture'.
>
> I have always been fascinated by what architects do with houses when they are their own clients because it is a key to the balance between their egos and their humanity. I am also fascinated by unselfconscious architecture without architects, such as the semi-detached builder's house, since it is a touchstone of everyday houses that make up most of our built environment.

At that point I wanted to cheer. It made such a change from the usual architectural snootiness. Elsewhere in the book however, Farrell does go a bit full-on architect,

> Reflecting on my own experience at my house in Ashworth Road, Maida Vale ... I realised that the way I occupied it and changed it and turned it around over the years was all about making a city, a world inside my own home. But equally the city reflects in its streets the halls and corridors and circulation of a house.

I think I know what he means, although given how few Londoners occupy entire houses, and given that you can currently pay three or four million pounds for a house in Ashworth Road, it may not be something many of us can share directly. If we want something even vaguely resembling the experience Farrell describes, we probably have to move out of central London to the 'real' suburbs, the affordable suburbs. Then, having moved out of the city, we might have a house to ourselves and explore the ways in which it may, or may not, be like a city, or a world.

Farrell would find plenty of support in *Dunroamin: The Suburban Semi and its Enemies* by Paul Oliver, Ian Davis and Ian Bentley (1981), which offers a convincing explanation for why architects hate suburbia so much.

> The main reason for the relentless hostility could have been that architects and planners were impotent as the growth of the suburbs continued remorselessly, largely without their designs and certainly despite all their criticism. Since this self-appointed elite could not stop the houses being built they were left to abuse the developers, builders and occupiers – a process that released their frustrations and retained their essential distance from the vast humanity beneath them.

Another supporter, and a professional writer on architecture and planning, was J.B. Jackson, founder and editor of the journal *Landscape*. There's an essay of his titled 'The Many Guises of Suburbia' in which he describes a 'kind of community' located by itself in the midst of farmland, where every family has much the same income, the same schooling, the same religious background, the same way of life, a place where there are few if any jobs and very little commercial life, with 'no cultural life in the urban meaning of the term'. 'Outsiders visiting the place are usually appalled by it.' Then he writes:

If the reader has identified this community as being an approximation of the average middle-class American suburb he will have been correct: but he will also have been correct if he identified it as a Southwestern Indian pueblo or a Chinese farm village or an Italian village like Silone's *Fontamara*, or a farm community in Eastern Europe or Asia or Latin America.

He concludes that we might think again about the suburbs we're familiar with 'and if we somehow learned to see them as belated American versions of an ancient and relatively world-wide community form instead of as land-speculation-induced nightmares, we might adjust to them a little more gracefully and intelligently than we are doing now.' Of course this raises a few questions about who exactly is a member of this 'we', and I suppose he means the professional architectural and 'planning community' of which he's a member, albeit a dissenting one. However, since the essay was written in 1961, we might think his hopes for a graceful and intelligent adjustment may have been lost, though not in the case of D.J. (Donald) Waldie, one of the great celebrants of California suburbia and author of the very personal and sometimes very poetic *Holy Land: A Suburban Memoir* (1996, revised 2005).

The book is a chronicle of his life in the community of Lakewood, and also a chronicle of Lakewood itself, a place that's usually regarded as a suburb of Los Angeles, though adminis-tratively it's a city in its own right. Waldie grew up there, and stayed there as an adult, working as an administrator in local government while living in the tract house his parents had bought in 1954.

He writes,

I continue to live here because I want to know what happens next in stories I think I already know. Loyalty is

the last habit that more sophisticated consumers would
impute to those of us who live here, we're supposed to
be so dissatisfied in the suburbs. But I'm not unusual
in living here for all the years I have. Perhaps like me,
my neighbours have found a place that permits restless
people to be still.

Waldie lived within walking distance of his job at City Hall,
and he tells the story of walking home from work at ten o clock
one Sunday night. Yes, he put in a lot of hours. As he walked,
a car slowed down ahead of him, pulled over and stopped. He
thought the driver was going to ask him for directions, but
instead a young man got out of the car, pointed a gun at Waldie's
chest and demanded his wallet. In a remarkable bit of strategy
or instinct Waldie said, 'I'm sorry, I don't understand you,' and
then fell slowly backwards onto the lawn of a nearby house. As
Waldie puts it, 'Nothing else happened. The porch light of the
house behind me came on. I heard the door of the car close;
I heard the car drive away.'

It's that sentence, 'Nothing else happened' that sounds so
very suburban and reassuring. Yes, this is an American story
that took place in an American suburb, and I imagine, without
being complacent, that nothing very similar is likely to happen
to me in my own Essex suburb but if by some chance it did, as
I was performing some nocturnal *flânerie*, and I was approached
by a man with a gun, I think that feigning incomprehension
and falling slowly backwards, hoping to trigger some security
lights on a neighbour's house, would be as good a plan as any.
I suppose handing over my wallet would be another possibility,
but we suburbanites, whether in California or Essex, are keen
to hold on to what's ours.

3

Some Suburban History

You'd think, wouldn't you, that somebody might have written a slim, elegant, concise volume on the history of suburbs and suburbia. It would very definitely have made my life much easier, but if somebody has written such a book, I've not been able to find it. As for other titles I've imagined – *The Encyclopedia of Suburbia* or *Everything You Ever Wanted to Know About the Suburbs* – apparently they're far too much to hope for. Therefore, what follows is a partial history that I've assembled patchily from various sources, scattered, fragmented and with a great many holes, no doubt, but as reliable as I can make it.

You'll find some, apparently quite serious, commentators who say the suburbs are a twentieth-century, even a post-Second World War, phenomenon. By any measure this is simply untrue. The history of the suburbs is essentially the history of cities. It's

very rare indeed to have a city without a suburb, and the logic
of the word suggests it wouldn't be possible to have a suburb
without a city, though that doesn't seem to be strictly true.

The city without a suburb might perhaps be one built inside
a sealed dome as in *The Simpsons Movie* or Stephen King's *Under
the Dome*, although suburbs would probably still grow up around
the perimeter of the dome. Or perhaps this suburb-free city
could be located in a place that's incredibly difficult to reach.
We assume there are no suburbs in Shangri-La or the Emerald
City, and if there are suburbs attached to any of the fifty-four
cities on Thomas More's island of Utopia, he doesn't see the
need to mention, much less describe, them. But these cities are
fictional. In the real world, chances are that wherever there's a
city there's likely to be a suburb or two.

The earliest cities appeared in Mesopotamia around 7500
BCE, when humans ceased to be hunter-gatherers and settled
down to engage in agriculture. Before long, cities were also
developing independently in other locations around the world.
Jericho, Damascus, Aleppo, Luouyang, Athens, Jerusalem, are
among the contenders for history's first city, but Uruk, settled
in the mid-fourth millennium BCE on the banks of the Tigris
(just downriver from Ur, Eriku and Babylon, all of which also
have some claims to be first), is the only one for which there
is existing physical evidence and written documentation (as
cuneiform texts) that date from the settlement's earliest times.

Uruk complicates matters by being a city state, but also
clarifies matters by being, for much of its history, a walled city.
Walls limit the size of the city, and therefore of the population.
Expansion requires a move outside the confines of the city. It
requires suburbs. The wall at Uruk, according to legend, was
built by Gilgamesh, and common sense suggests that you don't
go to the trouble of building a city wall unless you need one
for defence. Recent archaeological finds indicate that at one
time there were settlements, suburbs, outside Uruk's city walls,

and it's suggested that the suburban inhabitants at some point moved into the city when things became too dangerous and threatening in the outside world.

This back and forth is an ancient and ongoing pattern. Sometimes life in the city seems safe, pleasant, culturally rich, and so people move in. Then there are times when cities seem dangerous, impoverished, chaotic, and so people move out. There's nothing very surprising about this. But whereas we currently think of the suburbs as the province of the aspiring middle classes, and whereas they have at times been considered places of stews and malevolence, there have also been times when the suburbs were only for the very rich. In northern Iraq, in the second millennium BCE, there was the walled city of Nuzi. Outside the city walls was a tiny suburb consisting of just four large private houses, belonging to four very rich individuals. Now that's an exclusive suburb.

Once you start looking, ancient suburbs pop up everywhere. Tell Brak in northeastern Syria, despite being occupied from 6000 BCE onwards, is generally not considered to be a city at all, but rather a series of suburbs. The contradiction is obvious: how can there be a sub without an urbs? But archaeologists take a different view. There was even, from 2003–2006, an archaeological project with the glorious title *The Tell Brak Suburban Survey*.

In southern Mexico, archaeologists working on the ancient city of Izapa, at its peak between 700 and 1000 BCE, discovered what the American non-academic press described as ancient 'cookie-cutter' suburbs. The central city was surrounded by a network of forty or so smaller settlements, each with a ground plan that resembled that of the capital. This sounds uncannily, and satisfyingly, like Ebenezer Howard's plan for garden cities, of which more later.

Pestilence, however, does provide plot opportunities for writers. Boccaccio's *Decameron* (*c.* 1348–53) and Ben Jonson's *The Alchemist* (1610) both involve plagues and suburbs. In the former the storytellers leave Florence to avoid the plague in the city, and hole up in Fiesole, now if not then considered to be Florence's most exclusive and expensive suburb. In *The Alchemist* the master of the house, Lovewit, flees London, again to avoid the plague, leaving his servant Jeremy in charge; Jeremy becomes known as Face and is accused by his co-conspirator, Subtle, of having become a 'suburb-captain', i.e. an impersonator, not a real captain: an early suggestion that life in the suburbs is somehow inauthentic.

But let's concede that when we think of suburbs we don't immediately think of ancient Mesopotamia, the settlements of the Izapa empire, the outskirts of fourteenth century Florence or even seventeenth century London. According to John Archer in *Architecture and Suburbia* (2008), our current ideas about the individual, property, privacy, labour and selfhood were all impossible pre-Enlightenment, and he argues it was these new ideas that led to the invention of the single family house, and consequently to our notion of property ownership as a means of self-definition.

This strikes me as only partly persuasive. The concept, in one form or another, that an Englishman's home is his castle dates back to at least the sixteenth century. In 1567 the judge and legal scholar William Stanford wrote (in Anglo-Norman) in *Les Plees del Coron* (*The Pleas of the Crown*) that it was legal to kill a burglar in order to defend your house or your person. 'My house is to me as my castle.' (In the original, 'Ma measo e a moy: coe mo castel.')

But if the Enlightenment provided some theoretical ideas about privacy and home ownership, it was the Industrial Revolution that put them into practice. The Industrial Revolution changed the nature and size of cities, and therefore the nature of suburbs. From the middle of the eighteenth century onwards, industry increasingly drew vast numbers of people into cities from rural areas, to work in often dangerous, polluted, overcrowded and potentially lethal environments. These people lived where they worked. Would the workers have liked to leave the city at the end of a hard day and return to some clean, bucolic suburbs? No doubt many of them would, but such suburbs didn't exist and even if they had, there was no practical way for the workers to get in and out of the city on a daily basis. That required the growth of a comparatively wealthy middle class, combined with the spread of public transport.

In the United States there was the growth of the 'streetcar suburb'. The earliest ones used horse-drawn carriages, later replaced by trams or cable cars. Eventually there was also the railroad suburb. Llewellyn Park, in New Jersey, one of the very first planned suburbs, home to Thomas Edison, was designed as early as 1853, and was not only a railroad suburb but was also accessible by ferry.

Still, it was the train that made commuting widely possible, and this went hand in hand with suburbs being built for the commuters to live in, and so a kind of profitable symbiosis went on between the builders of railways and the builders of houses. In 1869, for instance, Frederick Olmstead and Calvert Vaux were commissioned to build a 'suburban village' on 1600 acres of land, nine miles west of Chicago. This became Riverside, and its location had everything to do with the route of the Chicago, Burlington and Quincy Railroad, which had been snaking out of Chicago since 1863. A local ordinance asserted that every house in Riverside had to have at least two trees in its front yard: environmentalism in the name of aesthetics, and perhaps the reverse.

1863 was also the year that the Metropolitan Railway began its operations in London, initially running a short line between Paddington and Farringdon, neither of those places being conspicuously suburban, but gradually the line extended northwest, sometimes underground, sometimes above ground, and by 1887 it extended all the way to Aylesbury, Buckinghamshire.

Not long after this time, a key figure emerges: Ebenezer Howard, the father of the Garden City Movement. It's surprisingly hard to reduce the concept of the Garden City to just a few words, Howard himself couldn't quite manage it, though he did write as follows, in his book *Garden Cities of To-Morrow: A Peaceful Path to Real Reform* (1898): 'Its object is, in short, to raise the standard of health and comfort of all true workers of whatever grade – the means by which these objects are to be achieved being a healthy, natural, and economic combination of town and country life, and this on land owned by the municipality.'

Howard's ideas did not come out of nowhere: Charles Fourier, William Morris, Henry Solly, had all written about idealised, planned communities, and Howard would also have been aware of the planned industrial villages at Bourneville, Port Sunlight and Saltaire. His triumph was to combine theory and practice. Within five years of publishing *Garden Cities of To-Morrow*, he had founded Letchworth Garden City, a real and thriving, if sometimes mocked, Utopian community.

Meanwhile, the Metropolitan Railway was continuing its suburban reach. This was a commercial rather than Utopian project. Having acquired land for the railway to run on, the Metropolitan, unlike many other railway companies, was allowed to retain ownership of any surplus. Suburbs were developed on this land, conveniently close to railway lines and stations, and these suburbs were given names such as Wembley Park, Willesden Park, Cecil Park, the Grange Estate, Cedars Estate or Harrow Garden Village, making them sound like bucolic idylls rather than suburbs.

Expansion was only somewhat curtailed by the First World War. It was in the midst of the war, in 1915, that the name Metro-land was created by the publicity department of Metropolitan Railways. From then until 1932 *Metro-land* was also the title of an annual publication, a piece of promotional literature posing as a tourist guide, extolling the area both as a place to visit and to live. In due course the name invoked a kind of nostalgia, often associated with John Betjeman, who in the 1973 BBC documentary *Metro-Land* recited the lines,

We laid our schemes, lured by the lush brochure,
Down byways beckoned, to build at last the cottage of our
    dreams,
A city clerk turned countryman again, and linked to the
    Metropolis by train.

However, if the Great War didn't hamper the plans of the
Metropolitan Railway, elsewhere in Britain it changed everything.
1919 was the year of the Addison Act, officially the Housing
and Town Planning Act, the legislation required to put into
practice Lloyd George's promise to create homes for heroes.
The Act provided local councils with subsidies to build houses
in areas of high demand, with an aim of building half a million
new houses, and although that target was never reached under
the act, further legislation meant that by the 1930s there were
over a million council-subsidised new homes, generally built as
suburbs on the edges of existing cities. My father's parents lived
in one of them in Sheffield: Firth Park.

Although there was some self-congratulation in Britain
in 2019 to celebrate a hundred years of public housing, it
was pointed out that New Zealand had got there some time
earlier, becoming the first Western country to provide public
housing for its citizens, under the Workers Dwelling Act of
1905. The New Zealand government built and rented out
'workmen's homes', high-quality houses, with large gardens,
on the outskirts of the main cities. There was a significant
political element to this. In 1919 an Auckland town planner
offered the opinion that,

> If a decent man is unable to secure a home for himself
> and his family, he is liable to become Bolshevik in his
> ideas and a menace to the community … [in the inner
> cities] small houses have been packed together to the
> extent of twenty-nine to the acre … is there any wonder

that under such conditions unrest and even disloyalty manifest themselves so frequently?

However, the New Zealand experience was less than a complete success. The rents were higher than many workmen could afford, many of the houses were beyond the reach of public transport, and eventually the properties were sold off to private landlords.

Back in Britain, between the wars, the combination of private and public building resulted in the creation of nearly three million new houses, the vast majority being what we would call suburban. The Second World War ended this, and afterwards, again with a vast housing shortage, the creation of suburban enclaves on the edges of existing cities wasn't enough. New Towns had to be built. By their own definition, these were not suburbs, and yet I think most people walking through many of the streets of Hitchin or Crawley, Reddich or Runcorn might be forgiven for thinking they were in deepest suburbia.

Australia, we're led to believe, not least by Jan Morris, had long been a country of suburbs. Perhaps this is not so surprising. Australia had a lot of space and a comparatively small population, so until recently sprawl didn't seem to be much of an issue, perhaps because the bush land around cities was not much valued. In Morris's book *Sydney* (2010), she tells us that in 1836 Charles Darwin compared the entire city to a London suburb, and that the suburbs of Sydney became more populous than the city itself as early as 1900.

> This is pre-eminently a city of suburbs, [she writes] *the* city of suburbs, perhaps; a city which has had whole books written about its suburbs, architectural studies of its suburbs, social analyses of its suburbs, suburban Governments, suburban styles, suburban loyalties and intense suburban prides.

Suburbia came naturally to Sydney. There is no denying that many city suburbs are less than lovely, their plans tedious, their streets (as Lawrence* thought) like children's drawings – 'little square bungalows dot-dot-dot …' I can see that socially progressive architects and planners must detest them. Nevertheless they represent for several hundred thousand people of many national origins, true human fulfilment – the very antithesis of the crowded tenements from which so many of their forebears came. Besides, they often turn out to be more interesting than you expect …

Even so, I think the most famous Australian suburb is not in Sydney but in Melbourne, Moonee Ponds, the real world home of the fictional Dame Edna Everage: 'The name means "a meeting of the waters", all Aboriginal words mean that.'† The place was archetypal no doubt, but chiefly chosen by Barry Humphreys because of its name I suspect, and the received wisdom is that Moonee Ponds has now become quite the gentrified and hipsterised suburb. Humphreys actually grew up in Camberwell, also in Melbourne but an affluent garden suburb, named after the considerably less affluent Camberwell in London.

Postwar Australian suburbs show a curious but appealing mix of American and British architectural influences, brick bungalows that are trying to look like cottages alongside California-style ranch houses. In Peter Cuffley's book *Australian Houses of the Forties and Fifties* (1993) – he also wrote a book titled *Australian Houses of the Twenties and Thirties* – he quotes a 1944 study titled *We Must Go On: A Study in Planned Reconstruction*

---

* That's D.H. Lawrence.

† That's from a Dame Edna routine, and seems to be partly accurate. The original Mone Mone Creek was a series of waterholes, but the name may derive from the Aboriginal word for lizard, or from John Moonee who was an early landowner in the area.

and Housing by Barnett, Burt and Heath. This called for half a million houses to be built within a decade, a figure that was in fact exceeded. However, in much the same time period 860,000 new immigrants arrived in Australia – Morris's 'many national origins.' They too needed housing, and at least some of them went to the suburbs, which made Australian suburbs, if not exactly intentionally, more integrated than many equivalents around the world.

If recognisable modern suburbs sprang up at about the same time in both Britain and the United States, the latter soon moved ahead in terms of size and numbers. Of course, it's got a lot to do with the United States being a bigger country, with having plenty of space and a bigger population and therefore economies of scale, but I think it has even more to do with automobile ownership, and especially with the business success of Henry Ford.

He wasn't an inventor, not even of the automobile assembly line – that honour goes to Ransom E. Olds of Oldsmobile – but Ford was the first to use that technology to create a car that was affordable by large numbers of 'ordinary' people. Car owners could live beyond the reach of public transport. They could live anywhere within 'driving distance' of work, and these distances became greater with the building of highways and freeways. Nobody wanted a punishingly long drive to and from work but there was, and for most commuters there still is, a trade off to be made between time spent travelling and the desirability of the suburban home at journey's end.

Robert E. Stern writes, 'It was Los Angeles which perfected the peculiarly American way of thinking of space in terms of time, time in terms of route.' This may well be true, but the equation of time, space and route now seems universal, certainly employed in Britain as much as in America. When British builders and estate agents advertise modern developments, the ads regularly proclaim 'only 20 minutes from Liverpool Street', 'convenient for the M62', and so on.

Even so, there's no British equivalent of Levittown, a development initially of 2000 detached houses, created on Long Island, New York between 1947 and 1951, just 25 miles from Manhattan. It's the all-American ur-suburb, the archetype, the prototype, the stereotype, of a certain kind of planned and prefabricated suburb. For that matter there is no British equivalent of William Levitt, the president and figurehead of the company that created Levittown in the family name: his father was the founder, brother Alfred was the planner and chief architect. William proudly said, 'We are not builders. We are manufacturers,' claiming that his company was 'the General Motors of the housing industry'. Not the Ford, note. At one point, the publicity had it, a new house was being finished every sixteen minutes at Levittown. George Wimpey and Lawrie Barrett were never in the same league.

From the air Levittown looks fabulous, a series of geometrical patterns resembling amoeba, cells, arteries. On the ground the designs don't look exactly inspired but they're no worse than in later and supposedly better-planned suburbs. For all their cheapness, the houses have lasted pretty well, many with recent modifications and refurbishments, of course.

Levittown's existence is intimately connected with America's 1948 Housing Bill, a piece of legislation that some sources consider 'socialist', which opened up billions of dollars in credit, allowing millions of Americans to take out five-percent-down, 30-year mortgages. Low repayments meant that a house in the suburbs could cost less than a small apartment in New York City. Many of the first inhabitants of Levittown were veterans returning from World War II, more heroes looking for homes, and in Levittown they didn't even have to put down a deposit. The Levitts built six more suburbs, some of them also called Levittown some not: one in Pennsylvania, one in New Jersey, three in Maryland and one in Puerto Rico.

A belief in the alleged socialist principles of Levittown is hard to sustain. William Levitt said, in words that would have made perfect sense to that New Zealand town planner some decades earlier, 'No one who owns his own house and lot can be a communist. He has too much to do.' On the surface this might mean that the suburbanite would be too busy mowing the lawn, clearing the gutters, redecorating the spare bedroom and so on, to do much political theorising. The subtext is that once suburbanites have a home of their own they have too much to *lose*. The property owner has a certain amount of wealth and capital that he doesn't want to see redistributed. The lesson was not lost on Margaret Thatcher.

There were also some noxious racial politics in Levittown. The standard lease contained a restrictive covenant stating that houses could not 'be used or occupied by any person other than members of the Caucasian race'. Since the Levitts were themselves Jewish this may at first look like a brutal commercial decision or even a matter of self-laceration. But in reality the restrictive covenant wasn't to keep out Jews, who moved there in considerable numbers, it was to keep out African Americans. The clause was eventually struck down, and in 1957, William and Daisy Myers, a Black couple with a young family, bought a house in Levittown, Pennsylvania. The people who sold it to them were Jewish: go pick the racial niceties out of that one. The Myers faced harassment, threats of violence, and on occasions an angry mob outside their front door. Nevertheless they stayed. They outlasted the mob, and filed criminal charges against their worst tormentors.

There's plenty of documentary evidence of what went on there, photographs, films, interviews. Some of it looks much like the usual sixties, racially-motivated violence, but in the interviews some of the inhabitants of Levittown, most of them women it must be said, show an empathy and an acceptance that seems many decades ahead of its time. Even so Levittown,

Pennsylvania has not become a deeply 'mixed' community. The 2010 Census recorded a Black population there of just 0.9%.

While integration was still being fiercely resisted in parts of America, a number of African American, middle-class suburbs were also being developed around the country. The currently most famous of these is Pontchartrain Park, in New Orleans, Louisiana.

It was built between 1955 and 1961 and was never large, but it did have a public park at its centre to serve the city's entire African American population. It also had a golf club. Wendell Pierce, the actor, one of the stars of the TV series *The Wire*, was raised there, and after the city and suburb was devastated by Hurricane Katrina in 2005, he was intensely involved in restoring the place, not without a struggle. His book *The Wind in the Reeds: A Storm, a Play and a City* (2016) describes his many difficulties. Even so,

> slowly but steadily, we are moving families into houses. For the first time, we have four or five white families living in Pontchartrain Park. In 2014 the basketball coach at the University of New Orleans bought a house in the neighborhood. My father's reaction? 'This is America, man, this is what it's all about.' I never thought I'd see the day when an 89-year-old Black man would be so happy to have a young white basketball coach and his family move into the neighborhood, and to declare that this liberty is what he fought for.

That's what we call suburban integration.

Increasingly in the second half of the twentieth century and into the twenty-first, certain attitudes have hardened against suburbia. I think it had something to do with 'the Sixties'. One of the many things that open-ended decade did was to create an 'us and them' mentality, a development of post-Second World War attitudes. Many of those who survived the hostilities, either in the military or as civilians, aka the 'older generation', were content to live a quiet post-war existence. They'd had enough 'excitement' to last them a lifetime. They wanted to get a job for life, raise children and be house proud. Suburbia suited them just fine. The comfortable progeny of that generation wanted something different and something 'more'. From their point of view, 'we' were hip, 'they' were square. 'We' were exciting and idealistic, 'they' were dull and cynical. 'We' were anti-war, anti-materialist, anti-capitalist, pro-free love, 'they' were just old fogies. At the time I liked to consider myself one of the 'we'.

One version of the sixties, countercultural dream involved living in a rustic commune in the middle of nowhere, and even if that was rarely realised or realisable, it still existed as the ideal. Even if you couldn't manage that, there were a great many options before you settled for living in suburbia.

In due course, inevitably, a lot of would-be hippies changed their behaviour, and possibly their minds. Attitudes softened once the realities of making a living and raising children arrived, and maybe that generation came to understand their own parents a little better. But the hippies' and the hipsters' dislike of suburbia didn't go away. Suburbia was still square and *for* squares – and if by some force of circumstances you found yourself living there, there was a need to distance yourself, to insist that you weren't like the neighbours, that you really didn't belong there. I don't claim to be entirely innocent of this.

Currently the division between 'us' and 'them' seems to be about something else. 'We' want to protect the environment and save the planet, 'they' want to drive diesel cars and use plastic straws. The pro-environment argument is an anti-sub-urban one. The suburbs are responsible for that terrible thing we now call sprawl. American suburbs tend to sprawl far more than British ones, simply because they have more room to do so. Defining sprawl may be as hard as defining a suburb, but Dolores Hayden offers this: 'a process of large-scale real estate development resulting in low density, scattered, discontinuous car-dependent construction usually on the periphery of declining older suburbs and shrinking city centers.' That describes the American model better than it does the English one, but the principle is much the same.

In fact, in England Ian Nairn was fretting about sprawl, without using the word, as early as June 1955 when he wrote the whole of a special issue of the *Architectural Review*, and titled it 'Outrage'.* He wrote, 'The Outrage is that the whole land surface is being covered by the creeping mildew that already surrounds all our towns. This death by slow decay we have called Subtopia, a compound word formed from suburb and utopia: i.e. making an ideal of suburbia.' The word also evokes the sense that this was a substandard kind of utopia. His deeper objection was to homogenization, a fear that everywhere in Britain was starting to look exactly the same, right down to the street furniture.

He asks the suburbanite to consider his own home (he assumes his reader has to be male)

'Is it still *rus in urbe*? (country in the city). Are you living in a true suburb or just a bit of spec builders' quick profit making?

'Can you take a country walk?

'Can your wife walk to the shops or is it a fag without a car?'

'Subtopia,' he tells us, 'is the annihilation of the site, the steamrolling of all individual places to one uniform and mediocre pattern,' and a large part of his concern is the disappearance of

---

* Curiously, or not, 1955 was also the year that Duncan Sandys, the Minister for Housing and Local Government, said in the House of Commons, 'I am convinced that, for the well-being of our people and for the preservation of the countryside, we have a clear duty to do all we can to prevent further unrestricted sprawl of the great cities.' I believe it's the first time a British politician publicly used the word sprawl and I'm grateful to John Grindrod's book *Outskirts* for this bit of information.

the countryside. He says, 'Britain has a population of 50,000,000 crammed into an island which could take 25,000,000 decently.' He doesn't make any recommendations for population control, though the inference seems obvious enough.

Lawrence A. Herzog in *Global Suburbs: Urban Sprawl from the Rio Grande to Rio de Janiero* (2015) makes as good a case as any for what's currently considered so bad about sprawl. When a book has sprawl in the title you can be certain that the contents are going to be anti-suburb. If I tell you there's a chapter titled 'Sprawl Kills: Ecological Crisis on the Urban Periphery' you'll get the idea. He writes: 'For over half a century, the American suburb was viewed as one of the nation's supreme achievements in modernist twentieth-century design,' though presumably not by him. One of his broader complaints is that the model of the American suburb has been exported to Central and South America, to locations and situations where it simply doesn't fit. He seems to have a point. He describes what he calls the mega-suburbs of São Paolo, Brazil. Like many high-end suburbs, these are gated communities, but within these gates the suburbanites live not in detached or semi-detached houses, but in massive high-rise tower blocks, which many of us might think prevents them being considered suburbs at all.

I have never seen one of these, except in pictures, but I have I friend (Richard Lapper formerly of the *Financial Times*) whose brother-in-law lives in one, in Vila Andrade, Jardin Morumbi, which consists of a dozen or so tower blocks clustered around a central area with a large swimming pool. In addition each tower also has its own pool. Richard's brother-in-law just happens to be a swimming-pool salesman.

It would be hard to accuse this development of sprawling in the usual sense, since a huge number of people are packed into a comparatively small area. Yet Herzog's main objections to sprawl remain, that it eats up and destroys the green environment, isolates individuals and communities. His solution is something he calls 'slow urbanism', a blend of Buddhist 'mindfulness', a connection with nature, and a high population density. This strikes me as a tough sell, and not only in suburbia.

China offers a different model, or rather a series of competing models. The 1990s saw a massive migration from the Chinese countryside to the cities, and the Chinese suburbs became a test lab for various styles of architecture, and various ways of living. One model features Le Corbusian 'towers in a park', which seem not to be especially popular: the towers are cramped, the parks are neglected, and these have in turn led to an appetite for American-style suburbs.

Bianca Bosker, the author of *Original Copies: Architectural Mimicry in Contemporary China* (2013), described some of the issues and one of the suburbs in an article in the *Guardian*, titled 'Why haven't China's cities learned from America's mistakes?' She writes:

> You'll find the original Rancho Santa Fe community nestled between golf courses and tennis clubs in sunny southern California. The version of it that I know best, however, is in the suburbs of Shanghai: this themed Chinese subdivision, modeled on the posh Californian suburb, features the same Mission-style homes with red tile roofs and the same lush green lawns encircling driveways mounted with basketball nets. There's at least one car in each garage, terracotta planters overflowing with flowers, and a clubhouse with tennis courts and swimming pools to soothe the stress of a long day at the office. And just in case the connection isn't clear enough, China's neighbourhood even has a familiar name: its developers called it 'Rancho Santa Fe.'

There might be certain other objections to using Rancho Santa Fe as a blueprint for living, let alone as a name. In 1996 members of the Heaven's Gate religious cult started renting a mansion inside the Californian version, near San Diego; it's a gated community. On 26 March 1997, the bodies of thirty-nine group members were found in the house, a mass suicide. Even so, local real-estate agents continue to list properties in Rancho Santa Fe as 'coveted'.

Many Japanese suburbs also imitate the American model, though it's not always an especially accurate imitation. A lot of what I know about Japanese suburbia comes from Cécile Asanuma-Brice, a sociologist living in Japan, and from her book, written in French, *Un Siècle de Banlieue Japonaise* (A Century of Japanese Suburbs), 2019. The title itself is significant. The French word *banlieue* signifies the *lieu*, the area outside of towns where the inhabitants were subject to a tax, a *ban*, so a suburb in France was originally an area defined by its tax status. That was never the pattern in Japan, where the word for suburb is *kôgai*, which Asanuma-Brice says is an in-between term, describing the way the city encroaches on the countryside thus making the countryside more urban. It also contains the *meishos*, places where people go to enjoy themselves, so the *kôgai* is a piece of countryside near the city.

Japanese suburbs that even vaguely resemble Western forms only became possible after the Meiji Restoration and the opening up of the country to international trade in 1868. At that point Japan looked to European industrialised countries for a way of proceeding. The garden city as imagined by Ebenezer Howard or the Familistère in Guise, northern France, were an influence, and in due course Japanese study groups were sent to investigate working-class housing in early twentieth century Europe. Japan consequently had its model suburbs, most successfully, says Asanuma-Brice at Manjû Kôba in Kurashiki, developed in the 1930s.

As with the Metropolitan Line in London, Japanese railway lines were extended outwards, then land was sold to developers to build houses for commuters. But it was after World War II that Japanese suburbs were increasingly built on the American model.

Asanuma-Brice is understandably sniffy about this, citing and criticising the Japanese suburbs as evidence of the spread of American capitalism and consumerism; which of course is also to criticise suburbs the world over. And yet the suburbs depicted in the photographs in her book strike me, in the main, as attractive and appealing places, and yes passing strange. I find it hard to think of them as some kind of globalised hell, though no doubt some people might.

Another source for my idea of the look of the Japanese suburbs (in addition to some days spent walking haphazardly and usually lost in the fringes of Tokyo*) is a book of photographs by Takashi Homma, titled *Tokyo Suburbia* (1998), with texts by the architect Momoyo Kaijima and the sociologist Shinji Miyada. It's a wonderful collection of photographs in which the suburbs look simultaneously familiar and alien: clusters of lookalike houses that you might possibly see in an English suburb, though probably wouldn't, some Macmansions, the occasional tower block, bursts of non-native flora, a few fast-food outlets, and kids who look callow and disaffected.

Japan also has a couple of local cultural problems to deal with. First there is a shrinking population, fewer young people, more older people, which means that there would, in any circumstances, be an over-supply of housing. Secondly, however, until recently most domestic buildings in Japan, and quite a few other types of building too, were not expected to last more than thirty years. If you bought an older house it was customary to demolish it and build a new house on the site. Demolition was one of the accepted expenses of acquiring a new home, as was employing an architect, so the existing

---

* One of my best memories is of a suburban walk I did in (I'm reasonably sure) Ueno. At one point I was in a curving alley lined with concrete fences behind which were unseen gardens and barely visible houses, and I looked up and saw, rising above the low roofs in front of me, a large golden statue of the Buddha. It's not an experience you're likely to have in suburban Essex.

house had no value in itself, and was a liability as much as an asset. If you were a younger Japanese person who happened to inherit a house from your family, chances were you'd have no use for it; you wouldn't want to live in it, probably preferring to live in a tower block in an urban centre, and you almost certainly couldn't sell it. And so a lot of suburban houses sit empty, falling into ruin, and no doubt causing consternation to the neighbours. The most recent figures I've seen say there are eight million unoccupied dwellings in Japan, sometimes known as 'ghost homes'. In some places local government is subsidising or even paying for demolition, but using public funds to demolish private properties is as unpopular in Japan as it would anywhere else. Even so, this might be one way in which suburbs could 'naturally' shrink and die.

It takes a brave man to write confidently about the suburbs of Africa, therefore in what follows I'll be writing quite diffidently. The cities and therefore the suburbs of Africa are wildly diverse, from the affluent and often gated and Western-seeming suburbs, to what at the other extreme are often perceived as shanty towns.

In the literature one is likely to come across pronouncements such as this one from Claire Mercer's 'Landscapes of extended ruralisation: postcolonial suburbs in Dar es Salaam, Tanzania' (2016) published under the auspices of the Royal Geographical Society.

The present paper is motivated by the postcolonial impulse to disturb teleological narratives that locate modernity in the West, which then becomes the centre from which theory, and history, emanates (Bhabha 1994, Chakrabarty 2000). I argue that the postcolonial suburb is a useful concept to work with because it both disrupts established Eurocentric ways of seeing and it connects the geographies of the present to those of the past.

That seems fair enough. Using the analytical tools, and indeed vocabulary, of Western urbanism and planning to investigate non-Western communities is obviously suspect. Mercer's findings in Tanzania are wonderfully unexpected. She describes, for example, the life of Mama Thomas

> a retired civil servant and widow, [who] lived with her son in Mbezi Beach on formal planned land that she and her husband had acquired through the state in the 1970s. She also kept a modest house on Kilimanjaro on her husband's inherited land. The land in Mbezi was originally farmland, and before moving there the family had lived in a government flat in the city centre. Mama Thomas started to build there in the 1980s. She was glad to move out to the suburbs as she found living in the city noisy and the neighbours irritating. Moving to the suburbs also enabled her to use the land around the house as the *kihamba* (home garden) would be used on Kilimanjaro. She had a poultry project with a thousand chickens in a small modern pen behind the house, as well as a patch of banana palms reminiscent of the coffee-banana groves of the Kilimanjaro *kihamba* belt.*

This does not resemble the story of anybody who lives in a Western suburb, and among other things it confirms Mercer's observation that many African suburbs contain far more rural elements than their non-African equivalents. Another salient feature is the lack of overall organisation: many African suburbs grow up at the edge of the cities as self-builders buy land,

---

* As a matter of fact when I lived in suburban Los Angeles my garden did have a (strictly non-commercial) patch of banana plants, but local zoning laws would have prevented me from raising a thousand, or indeed any, chickens.

create single homes, and eventually create accumulations of low-density housing.

As for the global future of suburbia, even more diffidence is appropriate, but it seems to be inextricably linked to population growth. Here is Ann Forsyth in an article titled. 'Global suburbia and the transition century: Physical suburbs in the long term' (2013), published in *Urban Design International*.

> While projections assume that populations will increase in the near term, many 'middle' and 'low' projections also chart a challenging new course where sometime between the middle and end of the century a new trend will emerge – global population growth will slow and perhaps even stop. Population shrinkage is already being faced in some metropolitan areas, due to uneven patterns of investment, but may well become pervasive. Certainly even with a flat population people could move to locations with more opportunities and household size could drop, necessitating more building, but the last century's pattern of relentless expansion will slow. The world has been growing for the contemporary planning profession's entire history – and certainly for the briefer history of the contemporary form of urban design – this transition is a major change. Suburbs, which have often grown at the expense of core cities, will themselves shrink.

I can't imagine anyone, whether living inside or outside the suburbs, would think that was necessarily a bad thing.

As far as I can tell there is no publicly active pro-sprawl lobby. If there is, they certainly don't call themselves that, and they aren't writing academic monographs on the subject; but then they don't need to. Many of them are fully occupied planning and building new suburban developments.

You can, however, find those who defend sprawl in the name of individual freedom. If people want a big house on half an acre of land, and they can afford it, then who's to tell them they can't have it? The government? Some self-interested planning committee? Some professor at UCLA?

The counter argument goes that freedom is all very well as long as it does no harm, and the anti-sprawl, anti-suburb lobby argues that an endlessly expanding suburbia *does* do harm, to the local environment, to the individuals in suburbia, and then to the world at large. It's hard to disagree completely with that argument: nobody wants to see every square inch of the planet disappearing under ranch houses and semis, nobody wants six-lane motorways running to and from every town. However, in the end it seems to be an argument about how much is enough, and how much is too much.

Do the suburbs have a future? I don't know. Nobody really does. A lot of urbanists, architects and architectural theorists will tell you the suburbs are unsustainable, and if that's the case then by definition they won't be sustained, but we're not going to demolish the ones we currently have and replace them with blocks of flats, much less turn them back into fields, are we? Or are we?

I don't know that the world needs any *more* suburbs. Clearly, with the world's present growing population, not everybody on the planet is going to be able to live in a single-family home with its own patch of land. Only a few years ago it seemed possible that we had reached 'peak suburb'. A large number of planners, conservationists and architectural theorists were telling us that we ought to want to be urbanists. However, in a post-Covid world that no longer seems such an urgent or persuasive idea. It appears that the pandemic may have given the suburbs a new lease of life, as places of safety, security and voluntary social-distancing. How long that state of affairs is likely to continue is unknowable. Things that make us feel safe may not be very enduring.

If I had to guess, and I know I don't, I'd say sooner or later, at some point in the future, suburbs may seem quaint or retro, like prefabs or thatched cottages. Perhaps suburbs will become frozen, static, part of our heritage, achieving conservation and preservation status. They may become theme parks. Maybe then everybody will learn to love them. Maybe.

4

Sheffield: The Greenhill Far Away

It was early one Sunday afternoon, when I was about fourteen years old, that I looked out of the back window of our council house on the Longley Estate in Sheffield, and saw that my dad, who'd been working in the garden, was in the middle of an argument with the neighbour, a hod carrier for the Public Works Department, for which my dad also worked, though as a foreman carpenter. This small difference in working status may have had something to do with what followed.

I realise now, if I didn't then, that the neighbour was very drunk. The alcohol had made him angry and aggressive, and at a certain moment he came over the fence and took a swing at my dad. Dad dodged the fist, grabbed it, then grabbed the man, and the two of them ended up wrestling on the ground. I ran to the kitchen to tell my mum what was happening and we both went outside.

We didn't go to *watch* exactly, but nor did we try to stop the fight. I'm sure some families would have piled in, but we didn't do that either. By then the neighbour's head was under my dad's arm, where it could be, and was, punched repeatedly. Dad was very obviously winning the fight, and perhaps if he'd been losing we'd have reacted differently.

Well, the fight petered out, as most fights do, the police were called, and the constable who came round said my dad could be in some danger of being charged with actual bodily harm. On the other hand, said the constable, the neighbour had started it, and he was trespassing on my dad's property. This surprised me. Even at fourteen year old, I knew we were renters, tenants in thrall to the council, and the idea that our back garden constituted my dad's 'property' had never occurred to me, and it didn't seem really to fit the case.

My dad was not charged with actual bodily harm, nor was the neighbour charged with trespass, but as you can imagine, the incident curdled what little neighbourly goodwill had existed up to that point. And in retrospect it's clear to me now that this must have been the moment when my dad decided he'd had enough of being a council tenant. He decided that he would buy a house of his own in the suburbs.

The story starts a little before then. I was born on the kitchen table in my grandparents' rented terraced house in Hillsborough, a rough but striving part of Sheffield. The family history doesn't fill in the details of why I was born there and then. Did I arrive in an unexpected hurry? Was the kitchen table part of the plan all along? Or were the midwife and ambulance called and on their way, but I just couldn't wait for them? At this point there's nobody alive who can provide me with answers.

Hillsborough was an interesting place back then. It had steelworks (that employed the men), factories that made sweets and fizzy drinks (and employed the women). It had a lot of pubs, betting shops, pork butchers, a dog track and the Sheffield Wednesday football ground. You could stand outside the back door of my grandparents' house, on the tarmac yard, and listen to the roar of the football crowd less than a mile away, and depending on the nature of that roar you could tell when Wednesday had scored, when they'd had a near miss, when the other side had scored.

I lived in that house with my parents and grandparents until I was about four years old, at which point my parents were rehoused by the council, but my grandparents stayed there until they died, so I saw a lot of the house and the area. I realise now that Hillsborough was, and still is, by any definition, a suburb: a community within the city, self-contained to a degree, and quite separate from the city centre. But it had none of the features we currently associate, perhaps lazily, with suburbia: no semi-detached houses, no lawns, no garages, no conservatories. It was district of small, cheap, terraced houses, most of them rented, which is to say it was working-class suburb, a further confirmation that suburbs come in all shapes and sizes.

My parents had few, if any, social aspirations but naturally enough they wanted a place of their own. The council offered them a ground-floor maisonette in an area called Greenhill. I don't have many memories of that place, and I'm not sure exactly how long we lived there, though I know it wasn't long. I do recall that the estate had an unfinished feel to it. We had to walk down a cinder track to get to the bus stop, there were piles of builders' sand here and there and there were no shops: various grocery vans arrived at strategic times during the week.

However, I do have one intense memory from shortly after we moved in. I was young enough still to be riding a tricycle, and this made me a target. Some older lads asked, politely enough, if they could have a ride on my trike. In my innocence I said all right, and off they went. I never saw the boys again although some time later, when my dad came home from work, we went out to search for the missing tricycle, and we found it dumped in the water of a nearby ditch. Does this kind of thing happen in suburbia proper? In Hampstead Garden Suburb? In Surbiton? Well possibly it does, but you tend to think not.

The business of the tricycle was not in itself the reason why my parents wanted to move on, though it can't have helped. My mother always said it was because of the noisy upstairs neighbours – the main bedroom in the lower maisonette was directly below the living room in the maisonette above – a fairly obvious design flaw. My mother said she could never live in a flat, and she never did.

At that time it was comparatively easy to move from one council property to another if you could find somebody to swap with, and so we went to a council house in Firth Park, on the other side of the city, in Horninglow Road, an end-of-terrace house, so essentially semi-detached, which was considered a good thing. But there was a 'gennel', a pedestrian alley, running alongside the house, where dubious lads hung out at night. And so another move, this time to the middle of a row of three council houses on the Longley Estate. This was reckoned to be a very good area. The graduations that defined the comparative desirability of the various council estates around Sheffield tended to the Jesuitical, but they were real enough.

The Longley Estate I now see, was made up of clusters of houses, repeated designs, repeated configurations, some short terraces of three or five houses. I don't recall there being any semis, and of course there weren't any detached. Looking at a map of Sheffield it's clear that many of the council estates were built on a geometric plan which didn't always have much regard for the underlying ground, often using concentric or intersecting circles and semi-circles. Horninglow Road, I now discover, was a more or less continuous loop. The roads I walked in Longley, on the way to school, the library, the park or the local shop, I now see on maps could have been drawn with a ruler and protractor and very probably were. It seems odd to me now that I had no sense of the rigorous geometry of the streets when I lived there, perhaps even stranger that nobody ever pointed it out.

I also realise now that it's more than likely that the planners in the Sheffield Council had at least some acquaintance with the work of Ebenezer Howard and the ideals of the garden-suburb movement, with the social and political ideas of William Morris and John Ruskin, all of which meshed with the city's socialist tendencies.

At the junior school in Longley we used to sing the hymn that runs: 'There is a green hill far away without a city wall', written in 1848 by Cecil Frances Alexander. I knew we had lived in a place called Greenhill, and I was confused. The hymn of course is referring to Golgotha, though nobody ever explained that to us. And although I instinctively knew that it wasn't referring to the Greenhill council estate where I'd once lived, I couldn't make sense of the word 'without' in this context. I understood it to mean 'not having' rather than the opposite of within. And it was quite true, the Greenhill I knew *didn't* have a city wall, but why was this worth remarking on? There wasn't a city wall, anywhere in the city, though I now know, as discussed elsewhere in this book, that having a city wall is a very good way of creating suburbs.

Even at junior school I became aware that some of the other kids lived differently from the way I did: not in council houses but in houses their parents owned, or were at any rate paying a mortgage on. I didn't understand every nuance, although my mother subsequently told me that the mother of my friend Rob

Torry, whose dad ran his own building business, and lived in a substantial but unspectacular private house not more than a mile away, was reluctant to let Rob play with me because she thought I was a rough little tyke from the council estate. I wonder if my mother was demonstrating some of her own anxieties here, because I spent quite a bit of time in the Torry house, and Rob's mother helped us with our French homework. Perhaps Mrs Torry was trying to smooth off my rough edges.

I think a visitor from space, possibly even one from outside of Britain, would have had a hard time distinguishing between a Longley council house and a Longley private house, between our house and the Torrys'. Yes, theirs had a bigger garden and the house may have been somewhat bigger, but it didn't seem any grander. Maybe it had bay windows and a glass front door, but that was about all: the houses were very definitely of the same species, the same breed.

My parents lived happily for a good while in Everingham Close, Longley, but that all changed when a new set of neighbours moved in, among them the violent drunken hod carrier with whom my dad had a fight, the event that persuaded him to head for the suburbs.

My dad began to take all the overtime he could get, did some moonlighting that mostly involved putting in fitted wardrobes and dormer windows, no doubt for people better off than us, and in due course he was able put down a deposit, take out a mortgage, and buy his own house.

This was before the Thatcher government introduced the 'right to buy' policy for council tenants. For obvious reasons my parents would not have bought a house next to a violent drunk, but it was a time when a lot of working-class families were realising that they could afford to buy their own homes, so there was nothing especially unusual or wildly aspirational about it. It made financial sense, it was better than paying rent for ever, you ended up with a valuable asset once the mortgage was paid off, and there was definitely some hope of having a better class of neighbour.

Do neighbours in suburbia ever come to blows? I'm sure they do, but my dad had certainly had his last fist fight. That in itself might be thought reason enough for moving to the suburbs.

In fact, despite my father's urge to move the family out of our house in Longley there's a pretty reasonable argument that council housing estates, especially those built between, say the beginning of the twentieth century and the 1960s when tower blocks took over, are themselves a form of suburbia. Between the wars Sheffield built about 28,000 council homes – my dad had grown up in one. At least some of the estates were apparently referred to as 'cottage suburbs', though I think you'd go a long way in Sheffield before you heard any locals using that term. There was even a garden suburb of sorts, known as the Flower Estate, and to a limited extent there still is.

In 1900 Sheffield Corporation bought land in an area known as High Wincobank, which would have been walking distance from where my dad was raised, in Stubbin Lane. The Corporation then held a competition for the design of 'workmen's cottages' – similar competitions were going on around the country. The first winning designs proved too expensive, and subsequent designs resulted in cheaper and less architecturally interesting buildings. Parts of the original estate are still there, to be seen along Primrose Avenue, Heather Road and Foxglove Road, though they're surrounded by later, more ordinary-looking council houses.

Much of the housing was built to higher than minimum requirements, and this moved Alderman Jackson of the city council's anti-Labour opposition to describe the Sheffield's council tenants as 'the pampered pets of the Corporation', which was no doubt designed to cause resentment in those less pampered. However, I do not believe that any Sheffield council tenants, at any time, in any location, have every considered themselves pampered.

*

So perhaps my parents' move was simply from one kind of suburb to another. My parents bought themselves a perfectly nice, perfectly unexceptional, three-bedroom semi-detached house in Kirkby Avenue, in Gleadless, a perfectly nice, perfectly unexceptional suburb in the southeast of the city. There was a tiny garden at the front, and a more substantial one at the back, where I learned, not wholly unwillingly, to use a lawn-mower. There was a driveway to keep the car off the road. A mock cherry tree grew outside the house on the stretch of grass between the road and the pavement. The neighbours didn't steal your kid's tricycle or come round drunk, threatening to beat you up.

Our immediate neighbour, the one on the other side of our thin, party wall, played easy-listening standards on the electric organ and he could be heard quite clearly. I suspect my parents thought they were getting their own back when I started playing electric guitar, but there were never any complaints, much less a confrontation.

One of the perceived advantages of home ownership was that you could make changes to the structure, make additions and subtractions that wouldn't have been allowed in a council house. My dad began by building a brick garage complete with inspection pit at the end of the driveway, at the side of the house, leaving a gap of no more than four or five feet between the nearest corner of the garage and the corner of the house where the kitchen looked out over the garden. The house had a front door and a side door, but no back door as such: to get to the back garden you went out through the side door. It seemed no big deal. A few years later dad decided to extend the kitchen, but he couldn't extend it very far because it would have met with the garage, and then there'd have been no access to the back garden. Consequently the amount of room gained by the kitchen extension was very limited. It seemed a lot of work for very little advantage, and although I never heard my mother complain, it struck me even at the time as indicative of both my dad's priorities (car before cooking) and also his lack of forward planning.

Our new house was hardly utopian but it was just fine. I was a teenager by then and didn't give much thought to matters of property ownership, but I couldn't imagine ending up in a house like my parents'. For one thing, I was already anticipating a life as some kind of writer, and I assumed I might well spend much of my life starving in attics, or just conceivably living in unexpected comfort on the lower slopes of the Hollywood Hills.

By then my perspective was changing anyway. I was going to the 'posh' grammar school on the other side of the city, in Broomhill, a place regularly described with a quotation from John Betjeman as 'still the prettiest suburb in England', Did he really believe this? Well he probably did for a few moments, in 1961. He was being interviewed by the *Sheffield Telegraph and Morning Post*, and he actually said,

> I thought of the leafy district of Broomhill on the western heights of Sheffield, where gabled black stone houses rise above the ponticums* and holly, and private cast-iron lamp-posts light the gravelled drives. Greek, Italian, Gothic, they stand in winding tree-shaded roads, these handsome mansions of the Victorian industrialists who made their pile from steel and cutlery in the crowded mills below. They lived in what is still the prettiest suburb in England.

Some of these words were recycled five years later in a poem titled, 'An Edwardian Sunday, Broomhill, Sheffield', which strikes

---

* I had absolutely no idea what a ponticum was; it's a variety of evergreen rhododendrum, originally imported from Spain, Portugal and Asia Minor and very popular in British suburbs in the Victorian times. It's now condemned as an invasive species. Suburban enthusiasms are anything but stable.

me as, at the very least, a poem with one or two ironies. It starts out apparently describing the joys of the place but I think it soon becomes deeply critical:

> High dormers are rising
> So sharp and surprising,
> And ponticum edges
> The driveways of gravel;
> Stone houses from ledges
> Look down on ravines.

Those ravines, one of which he describes later in the poem as a 'chemical valley', are where the problems and the criticism lie. Those are the places where the wealth was created, where the industry and the work and the filth and pollution were located. The early inhabitants of Broomhill really did, in the geographical sense, look down on all that; they might think they were above it all, because topographically they were. But again it would have seemed to me then, if I'd thought about it, that Broomhill really didn't resemble my, or most people's, idea of suburbia. It was too well-off, too leafy, the houses bigger, too individualistic and older than we think of as suburban, plus there were hospitals, the boys' grammar school which I went to, and a girls' grammar school across the road. There were many university buildings, a botanic garden. The current Pevsner describes Broomhill as Sheffield's 'first middle-class suburb', which only clarifies things somewhat.

At the end of the school day, I often walked halfway home, by one circuitous route or another, which involved going down from Broomhill into the city centre. Broomhall was the red-light district and many schoolboys claimed to have met, talked to and received offers from prostitutes but I never heard that any of the lads did any business. I did however discover, as did the world, that one of the roads very close to my school in Broomhill,

Melbourne Avenue, one down which I regularly walked, was the place where Peter Sutcliffe, the Yorkshire Ripper, was eventually arrested, not because diligent policework had tracked him down as a rapist, but because his car had false number plates.

While my parents were alive I was a regular visitor to Sheffield, though these, of course, didn't count as field trips. After my parents died I inherited their house. I had a life in London, and a claustrophobic studio flat, at that time and had no use for a semi-detached house in Sheffield, though there have been times since when I've wondered how things might have turned out if I'd decided to sell up in London and become a Sheffield suburbanite. But I didn't. I sold the house, and my attachment to Sheffield became slighter.

I still had a few old friends in Sheffield and sometimes I went up to see them, but our lives were taking us in increasingly different directions, and so these trips became less frequent. But even when I did go back, the one thing I never thought of doing was making a sentimental journey to revisit my parents' old house. I'm not entirely sure why. Partly it seemed unnecessary. My parents were no longer there, and although I did have some happy memories of living in that house, I had some less good ones too, all concerned with the difficulties of adolescence, and if by any chance I wanted to revisit those memories, I could do it without physically revisiting the bricks and mortar of the house.

But recently, since I was writing a book about suburbia, I decided to go back and try to look at the old house and the neighbourhood with new as well as old eyes. I honestly didn't know how it would feel. Would there be torrents of warm emotion, or would it just be painful? Or would I feel nothing at all, and might that indicate some emotional fault and deadness in me?

I spent a long weekend in Sheffield, didn't tell any of my few remaining friends and relatives that I was coming. I stayed in a hotel in the middle of town and I went to Gleadless by bus, the 51, which was the one I'd always used, though the route had changed a little. The bus went out from the city centre, past the Sheffield United football ground, through Olive Grove,* up East Bank Road into the Arbourthorne Estate. We passed a multitude of what I would once have thought of as plain, typical council houses, but the estate agents' 'for sale' and 'sold' boards dotted around indicated that many were now in private hands.

I got off at Gleadless Common and, indirectly though not exactly stealthily, made my way through various calm, quiet suburban streets that led to Kirkby Avenue and my parents' old house. The neighborhood didn't seem any different from the way I remembered it, didn't appear to have gone up or down in the world. I passed one large, familiar, and exceptional house that had belonged to a local bookmaker; it had started out as an old stone house, part of the original Gleadless village, and it had been extended several times. The current incarnation included an upper-floor extension with a floor-to-ceiling glass wall and a carport underneath, which struck me as distinctly Californian. This was by far the biggest house in the neighbourhood, and the only flashy one. Otherwise the houses were neat, clean, well looked after, with nothing fancy or showy about them, which was just the way my parents would have wanted it. I did see one house near by where the owner had clipped his long yew hedge into the shape of a locomotive. I wasn't sure what my parents would have thought about that, though I was sure they'd have had an opinion. My guess was that they'd have thought it was silly, a needless bit of showing off.

---

* Was there ever an olive grove in Sheffield? It's just about possible. The area apparently gets its name from a house there called Olive Grove, and we all know how inscrutable house naming is. It's possible the occupier grew, or tried to grow, olives. Equally possible, the occupier may have been on some version of the Grand Tour and wanted to be reminded of warmer regions; or possibly it's a biblical reference. Sheffield scholars remain undecided.

I got to my parents' house and it looked very, very much as I remembered it; more so than I'd expected. I thought it might have seemed smaller than I remembered, pokier, more modest, but no, it still conformed to the mental image I had. It even had vertical slatted blinds on all the windows, just like the ones my mother had favoured.

The brickwork, the pebble dashing, the front garden, all seemed untouched, but there was one significant change. Someone, perhaps the current owner, perhaps a previous one, had extended the kitchen beyond my dad's original size, so that now the kitchen wall met the side of the garage and went beyond it, allowing no access at all to the back garden from the side of the house or the driveway. For that matter there was no *view* of the back garden either. There could have been anything going on back there – fountains, naked statuary, a grotto – though on balance I suspect not. Even so, it still seemed odd, and, thinking about it since, I imagine the builder must have a created a door in the side of the garage to provide a way through, so that to get to the garden you had to go through the garage. It would have solved the problem of the too-small kitchen, though again the advantage didn't seem huge. I expect my dad would have thought it was far too much trouble.

Did I experience any gush of uncontrollable emotion at the sight of the house? You know, I really didn't. I was ready to feel grief or anguish or melancholy, and I do sometimes feel those things when I think about the loss of my parents and the loss of the lives they led, but the mere material reality of their old house – which I never thought of as *my* old house – didn't bring out those feelings. If they'd lived in a grander house with more history, or perhaps in a smaller but homelier, quirkier place, somewhere with more personality, it might have been different. But this looked like any other suburban house. And perhaps on a different day, in different circumstances I'd have felt differently. It wasn't that I felt nothing at all, just that what

I felt, the nostalgia, the melancholy, the sense of loss, was severely muted. This was not the place for grand emotions. I wonder if my reaction was all too suburban.

5

Ebenezer's Good: The Garden and the Field

If you're a property developer, and you're building a brand new run-of-the-mill, but top-of-the-line, suburban estate on a green field site that's convenient for the motorway with first-class rail connections near by, it classes things up no end if your promotional literature says the design is based on the principles of Ebenezer Howard's Garden City Movement. This may or may not be true, but either way you're pretty safe. The people who are going to be interested in buying a house in your development are unlikely to be very familiar with these principles, which in any case are fairly amorphous, but 'garden city' sounds good and appealing in a non-specific kind of way. Most people have some affection for gardens, and the ones who don't are clearly not your market.

Ebenezer Howard (1850–1928) was indeed the father of the Garden City Movement, even if there had previously been historical examples of places that were garden cities in everything but name. He founded Letchworth Garden City in 1903, and then Welwyn Garden City in 1920. (A word to the wise: neither of these places is actually classified as a city, and Welwyn is sometimes considered a 'new town'.) He didn't call them Letchworth Garden Suburb or Welwyn Garden Suburb, but he might just as well have done. A garden city (the term was always a loose one, and has become looser over time) is in some sense a city of gardens, which is to say it's a city of suburbs, each suburb made up of individual dwellings, each with their own private patch of greenery. Of course, not everybody likes that idea. Jane Jacobs, in *The Death and Life of Great American Cities* (1961), denounced Howard in these terms, 'He focused on the provision of wholesome housing as the central problem to which everything else was subsidiary; furthermore he defined wholesomeness in terms only of suburban physical qualities and small-town social qualities.' Alan Barker, in *The Freedoms of Suburbia* (2009), says that Letchworth 'is really a planned suburb'. I'm sure Howard would have disagreed, but I assume he'd have shrugged off such criticisms.

He envisaged a way of life that combined the best aspects of living in the city with the best aspects of living in the country; not such a terrible aim. This diagram of his shows how it might possibly have worked:

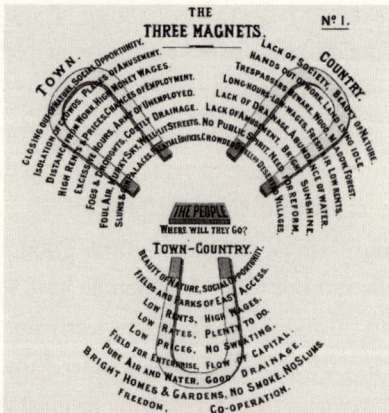

Howard was very keen on the country, and he assumed that everyone else was too. He wrote:

> Religious and political questions too often divide us into hostile camps; and so, in the very realms where calm, dispassionate thought and pure emotions are the essentials of all advance towards right beliefs and sound principles of action, the din of battle and the struggles of contending hosts are more forcibly suggested to the on-looker than the really sincere love of truth and love of country which, one may yet be sure, animate nearly all breasts.

A plain prose style was not for him, but he did have a point. Living conditions in the great industrial British cities at the end of the nineteenth century were certainly appalling, and moving people out of them was one solution. An alternative solution – to improve those living conditions and leave the people where they were – either never occurred to Howard, or perhaps he thought that was too big a task even for him.

Ebenezer Howard was born in London and educated at various private schools, but his formal education ended when he was fifteen and he did a variety of clerical jobs, for stockbrokers and solicitors, and eventually as private secretary to a preacher, Joseph Parker. At twenty-one he made a bold and unsuccessful attempt to become a farmer in Nebraska, but ended up as a stenographer in Chicago, where he would most likely have been aware of the work and town planning of Frederick Law Olmsted in the suburb of Riverside. In 1876 Howard came back to London to work as a scribe for Hansard before setting up a business of his own.

He seems to have read widely and been interested in social reform in a general way, absorbing the ideas of Ruskin, Morris, George Bernard Shaw, Sidney Webb and even Peter Kropotkin, a Russian prince who espoused anarcho-communism while living in the London suburbs of Harrow, Bromley and Mill Hill. And in 1889 Howard read a life-changing book. It was a novel by Edward Bellamy, published the previous year in the United States, titled *Looking Backward, 2000 to 1887*. A time traveller, as we might call him, from 1887, wakes up to find himself in his home town of Boston, but it's now the year 2000. With the help of wise and friendly locals of the future he compares conditions 'then and now'.

H.G. Wells's *The Time Machine* seems an obvious point of comparison, though that book wasn't published until seven years later, and I suspect Bellamy would have considered it rather too racy. And whereas Wells's novel, like the vast majority of novels set in the future, is essentially dystopian, Bellamy's is anything but. The new Boston his hero discovers is an absolute paradise, not least in the way it looks:

'Miles of broad streets, shaded by trees and lined with fine buildings, for the most part not in continuous blocks but set in larger or smaller inclosures, stretched in every direction. Every quarter contained large open squares filled with trees, among which statues glistened and fountains flashed in the late afternoon sun.' So far, so suburban, but then, 'Public buildings of a colossal size and an architectural grandeur unparalleled in my day raised their stately piles on every side' – which sounds a little too Albert Speer for me.

Bellamy's time traveller has discovered a very grand garden city, and, it turns out, one based on socialist principles. Here citizens cooperate, the free markets don't dominate, there's benign central planning, there's no war, no envy, no poverty, no prisons, no lawyers. Labour relations are harmonious, women are independent and fully emancipated. There's also a steampunk version of Amazon, with goods flowing into homes from a central warehouse via a system of pneumatic tubes. Sex is so well regulated as to seem a form of eugenics. The oiks don't get to breed. 'Of all the whips, and spurs, and baits, and prizes, there is none like the thought of the radiant faces which the laggards will find averted ...Celibates nowadays are almost invariably men who have failed to acquit themselves creditably in the work of life.' Today we call them incels.

Ebenezer Howard loved the book. He wrote:

> This I read at a sitting, not at all critically ... The next morning as I went up to the City from Stamford Hill I realised, as never before, the splendid possibilities of a new civilisation based on service to the community and not on self-interest, at present the dominant motive. Then I determined to take such part as I could, however small it might be, in helping to bring a new civilisation into being.

Howard always aimed high.

These days it seems to require rather more than an 'uncritical' reading in order to be taken in by *Looking Backward,* and to give Howard his due, he did come to see Bellamy's vision of the future as too authoritarian, though that took some time. Still, Howard was sincere enough in his desire to create a better world, and he promoted Bellamy's book, subsidising the publication of a British edition, but obviously that wasn't enough. He needed to write a book of his own, and he did. This was *Garden Cities of To-Morrow: A Peaceful Path to Real Reform* (1898), which was later reprinted in a revised version as *Garden Cities of To-morrow* (1902).

The word suburb occurs just once in the earlier edition, in relation to the improved rail service Howard envisages for linking one garden city to another, 'Those who have experience of the difficulty of getting from one suburb of London to another will see in a moment what an enormous advantage those who dwell in such a group of cities as here shown would enjoy, because they would have a railway *system* and not a railway *chaos* to serve their ends.'

Those words appear unchanged in the later edition but there's also now a quotation from John Ruskin's *Sesame and Lilies* (1865) which asks for, 'thorough sanitary and remedial action in the houses that we have; and then the building of more, strongly, beautifully, and in groups of limited extent, kept in proportion to their streams, and walled around, so that there may be no festering and wretched suburb anywhere.'

Howard's book is not, or at least not only, a utopian fantasy. It purports to be a thoroughly practical guide, explaining how a garden city might actually be built to his specifications in the real world. He explains,

> The reader is asked to imagine an estate embracing an area of 6,000 acres, which is at present purely agricultural, and has been obtained by purchase in the open market at a cost of £40 an acre, or £240,000. The purchase money is supposed to have been raised on mortgage debentures, bearing interest at an average rate not exceeding £4 per cent. The estate is legally vested in the names of four gentlemen of responsible position and of undoubted probity and honour, who hold it in trust, first, as a security for the debenture-holders, and, secondly, in trust for the people of Garden City, the Town-country magnet, which it is intended to build thereon.

And so on.

Howard further explains that the city trust would build houses for 30,000 people, in a residential area that would cover one sixth of those 6,000 acres (i.e. 30 people per acre – the kind of low density that would dismay modern urbanists), leaving the rest for agriculture. And although Howard did at least imagine a plan for an industrial zone where there'd be factories, and therefore presumably jobs, this insistence on the importance of agricultural employment seems a little out of touch even for

1899. He also imagined that the plan would be such a success
that eventually the government would step in and build garden
cities throughout the country.

Actually, the best thing about the books are the illustrations:
a kind of diagrammatic fantasy art. We've already seen Howard's
notion of magnets, but there are also maps of how a cluster of
garden cities might look. This kind of thing:

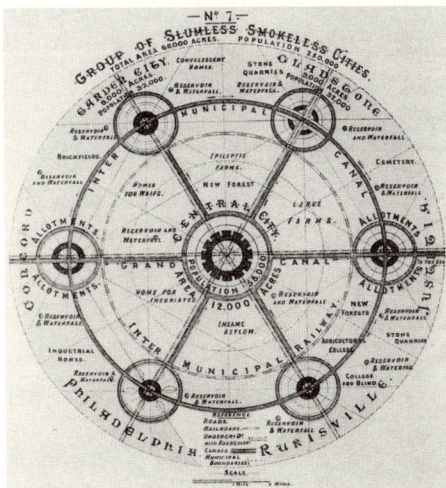

Some sources say that Howard never really imagined his cities
would be as schematic as this, but if that's the case, why didn't
he take his illustrator in hand and make him draw something
more realistic? The plan looks appealing, orderly, geometrical
and neat, and yes, Howard admits it's only a diagram, but it's
quite obviously neater than any real bit of territory would ever
be. It has a wayward relationship to any topography that could
exist in reality. It would apparently demand a flat plane, or plain,
an area without natural features such as broad rivers, high hills
or deep valleys, but then as you peer more closely and read the
small print on the diagrams you see that there are large numbers

of reservoirs and waterfalls all over the site. And then you see, scattered among the cities, there are to be homes for inebriates, insane asylums and epileptic farms (we can only guess how they would work). This seems a layout designed for a horror movie or a dodgy video game.

But the clustering itself, with its inevitable spread (or sprawl), is the main problem. Each group of seven slum-free, smokeless cities would, by Howard's account, have a population of 250,000. London's population in 1900 was 6.7 million, up from just one million a century earlier. So if Howard's plan had been a great success, if say a million people from London had decided they wanted to move out of the big smoke and live in a garden city, then four of these new city clusters, i.e. 28 brand new cities, would have had to be built. Since each of these clusters was to cover 66,000 acres, four of them would have covered 264,000 acres, more than 400 square miles, over 1000 square kilometers. Garden cities for 2 million would have covered 800 square miles, cities for 5 million would have covered 2000 square miles, and so on.

For comparison, at this density the current population of London, 8.7 million, would cover about 3,500 square miles, as opposed to the actual situation in which those 8.7 million occupy just 607 square miles. Howard's enterprise looks doomed, and the more successful it was, the greater the number of people who wanted to live in his garden cities, the more impossible the practicalities would have been.

You can't blame a man for being optimistic but you can blame him for being utterly unrealistic. Howard's plan sounds impossible, and in the ultimate sense it was – large numbers of garden cities were never built – but perhaps the most surprising and confounding thing of all is that a version of Howard's plan and his city did indeed come into existence, even if would never be part of the grand scheme he wanted.

In 1899 Howard founded the Garden City Association, to spread and publicise his ideas. In 1902 he set up the Garden

City Pioneer Company to find a suitable site on which a garden city could be built. It turned out to be a few thousand acres of Hertfordshire, not too far from London. This became Letchworth, which was the name of one of the villages in the area. And I do wonder how important that name was. Howard may have been a high-minded innocent, and some of the inhabitants of his garden city no doubt were too, but for the rest of us, doesn't that name Letchworth conjure up absurd visions of lechery and lechers? Doesn't it result in a certain amount of snickering from the lower orders? Not that the lower orders got much of a look in.

In 1903 Howard founded the First Garden City Company, which began organising the actual building of the city, with many of the financial arrangements much as he'd described in his books. There was then a competition to find planners for the city, following which Unwin and Parker (Raymond Unwin and Richard Barry Parker) were selected to be Chief Consulting Architects.

Unwin and Parker were an ideal choice, though Parker was more deeply involved with Letchworth than was Unwin. They had good socialist credentials. Unwin had been an engineer working on the design of buildings and housing for mining communities in Derbyshire, and while there, he'd been a member of the Sheffield Socialist League and of William Morris's Social League. Parker was more the aesthete, having studied art, architecture and furniture design, and once his education was finished he'd built houses for his bank-manager father.

The Unwin and Parker practice had built some individual houses in the Arts and Crafts style, and created pattern books that allowed other, less imaginative, architects to create Arts and Crafts homes. In 1902 they'd been commissioned to design a 'model village' for the Rowntree Brothers in New Earswick, near York. Michael Middleton, in *Man Made the Town* (1987), discusses of the 'company villages' of Bourneville, Saltaire and Port Sunlight. He writes, 'These paternalist communities for the working class were, in some measure, prototypes for the Garden City Movement – the voluntary, middle-class equivalent.' If Howard worried about paternalism he didn't show it.

There were further competitions: a Cheap Cottages Competition in 1905, another in 1907, with the winners actually being built. Other plans were slower to come to life. A town square was planned in 1910 but not operational till 1935. Howard envisaged a population of 30,000 for Letchworth, a number that was only achieved a good hundred years after the city's founding.

Middleton has a point about the social make up of garden cities. The population of Letchworth was always, however we choose to define it, primarily middle class. It was never cheap to live there and it certainly isn't now, but the place also gained a reputation for being a home to cranks, again defined in various different ways, though vegetarianism and maypole-dancing figure largely. This endeared it to certain people, not least George Bernard Shaw, and it famously did not endear it to George Orwell, who for a while lived near by.

He writes in *The Road to Wigan Pier* (1937):

> One day this summer I was riding through Letchworth when the bus stopped and two dreadful-looking old men got on to it. They were both about sixty, both very short, pink and chubby, and both hatless … They were dressed in pistachio-coloured shirts and khaki-shorts into which their huge bottoms were crammed so tightly that you could study every dimple. Their appearance created a mild stir of horror on top of the bus. The man next to me … murmured 'Socialists.'

Orwell concludes, 'He was probably right.'

If anyone is entitled to bad-mouth socialism it's surely George Orwell, and in the same book he did so. He says that socialism attracts 'with magnetic force every fruit-juice drinker, nudist, sandal-wearer, sex-maniac, Quaker, "Nature Cure" quack, pacifist and feminist in England'. He also includes an 'outer-suburban creeping Jesus'. That, by some accounts, pretty well describes the population of Letchworth Garden City, but I'm left wondering if a creeping Jesus from the *inner* suburbs would be more or less contemptible in Orwell's estimation.

The city's reputation for absurdity seems justified. For example, Howard liked the atmosphere of pubs, but he hated alcohol, and so he set up an alcohol-free pub. Letchworth officially stayed dry until 1961 when the city's first alcohol licence was issued to a hotel. The first pub serving alcohol didn't open until 1974, although it had been possible for some decades to get a drink at the local Conservative Club if you joined the Tory party.

There were contradictions too. You would imagine that suffragettes would have been welcomed with open arms in Letchworth, and to a considerable extent they were, but the story goes that when Howard encountered a couple of them walking barefoot across the common he told them they were a disgrace to their cause.

I decided to go on a field trip.

When you get off the train at Letchworth there's a large sign in the station, blue letters on a white background, telling you that you're in 'the world's first garden city'. It did then suddenly occur to me as I walked along the platform, that Babylon, with its hanging gardens, might have a prior claim to that title, but probably I was just being contrary. And if, on your field trip, you should walk all the way down Broadway, which is the main drag, to the southeastern end of things, there's another signpost hammering home the message. This one has a low-relief profile of Ebenezer Howard which makes him look benign but grouchy, complete with droopy mustache, a little like Yosemite Sam, the prospector in the Bugs Bunny cartoons.

The site of Letchworth Garden City is comparatively flat though not nearly as flat as Ebenezer Howard's diagram would have required – how could it be? – and there are no reservoirs with waterfalls, nor epileptic farms for that matter. And more to the point, although there's a certain pleasant geometry about the streets, they're by no means symmetrical. The Unwin and Parker scheme inevitably bears only a passing resemblance to Howard's idealised plan, and the evidence is that Parker never entirely bought into Howard's garden city ideals. In Letchworth the real world has intervened, to everybody's advantage, I'd say.

You walk out of the railway station and you're in the city centre, a pedestrian precinct with pubs and cafés, a serious, proper butcher, and there's an arcade, not the kind Howard imagined: he foresaw a continuous circular arcade that might curl around the whole city. It's even less the kind that Walter Benjamin was familiar with, but it's an arcade all right, with an art gallery that was showing an Eduardo Paolozzi exhibition when I was there.

At the end of the pedestrian walkway there's a central green, that's Broadway Gardens, rather too long and thin to be considered a square, and a few roads do radiate out from it, but not in a regular or uniform pattern, and outside of that area the roads and streets are no more orderly than roads and streets anywhere else.

This all felt quite small-town but it didn't feel especially suburban, and of course it was the suburbs that interested me. Fortunately for my purposes, the commercial centre is small and you soon find yourself in what feels like the suburbs whichever direction you go. Some of them are conspicuously fancier and less humble than others. A few looked like superior council houses, some were full-on Arts and Crafts extravaganzas. Some of the cottages built for the exhibitions in the early part of the twentieth century are still there, and labelled with plaques. Elsewhere some of the more recent and less prepossessing suburban developments are built right up against an industrial estate with the back garden walls as the boundary.

I walked and I wandered and I looked around me. I thought somebody might ask me what I was up to. I reckoned I had a good answer. I was planning to say that I was thinking about moving to Letchworth and was having a good look round – I thought that might produce all manner of information and anecdote – but nobody ever approached me to ask me anything. In other places they have done.

There were two things that struck me on this brief and inevitably superficial visit to Letchworth. First, the long sweeping roofs and rooflines on many of the houses. This was perhaps unsurprising on the more thoroughly Arts and Crafts houses, but these swoops were as likely to be seen on the more ordinary houses as well. I was reminded of ski jumps.

The other thing that stood out: although the street plan may not have been symmetrical, many of the buildings were, intensely so. Naturally enough the semi-detached houses tended to be mirror images of each other. I suppose somebody somewhere has built totally unmatching semi-detached houses, but I've never seen them. And perhaps it was not a huge surprise that the detached bungalows, and there were quite a few of those, were symmetrical in themselves, a door in the middle, windows, sometimes bay windows, at either side, sometimes with half-timbering above.

But there were places where two matching detached houses had been built side by side, symmetrical right down to the placement of the garages, which had been built in the gap between the two houses, on the left of one house, on the right of the other, so that the two garages were then attached, or semi-attached, to each other, to complete the effect.

Since I was in a garden city, I decided to take a closer look at the gardens. I wasn't expecting wild eccentricity but even so they were much tamer than I'd have imagined. Nobody was expressing themself through their garden as far as I could see. There were a few curious, interesting looking plants here and there, the owner of one patch had created what looked like a small market garden, with raised beds bearing large quantities of cabbages, leeks and sprouts. This, I think, would have pleased Ebenezer Howard, though I imagine he'd have been less pleased by the blue padded chair in the shape of a giant hand that was decaying in one of the other front gardens nearby. And I can't even imagine what he'd have made of a children's climbing frame on one front lawn that was in the shape of a geodesic dome.

Naturally enough there are also public gardens in Letchworth, not least those central Broadway Gardens, a name that was adopted at the time of the Letchworth centenary. For a while before that they were the John F. Kennedy Gardens – a fact memorialised by a large block of granite.

There are also Howard Park and Gardens, which contain an adventure playground, water features, a bowling green and a naked statue of Sappho – not every public garden has one of those. And for a good while Howard Park and Gardens didn't have one either. The statue was presented to the city in 1907 and moved around from one place to another until it was stolen in 1998. It was never found or returned, so what's there now is a replica. I saw it round about Poppy Day, and she was wearing a tiara made of red paper poppies.

The notion that Letchworth might be home to statue thieves would no doubt have appalled Ebenezer Howard, but then so would many other manifestations of modern life now to be seen in Letchworth. A man who was against alcohol would surely have taken against vaping, but there was a vape store right on the main street. And a man who got upset about barefooted women on the common would surely have had a fit at the presence of another of the businesses on the main drag: No Morals Tattoos. Vaping and getting tattoos may not be part of the garden city ideal, and they were once at the fringes of contemporary life and culture, but now they're as suburban as anything.

After the First World War, Ebenezer Howard was disappointed to find that even though the government was involved in the creation of vast amounts of new housing, they weren't (incredibly) following his garden city blueprint, so he decided to build another city himself. He bought 1500 or so acres, also in Hertfordshire, between London and Letchworth, a site that would become Welwyn Garden City, founded in 1920.

As before, Howard thought big but achieved limited results, and Welwyn was always going to be small potatoes compared with Letchworth. He imagined Welwyn would have a population of 42,000 but by 1930, two years after his death, the population was just over eight and a half thousand. It's easy, but probably unfair, to dismiss Howard as a dreamer. True, his reach was bigger than his grasp, his ambitions greater than anything he achieved, but he did build two 'cities'. Just how many people have ever done that?

Howard appointed a French-Canadian architect, Louis de Soissons, to be both architect and town planner of Welwyn, and in order to boost local morale, Howard moved there, to a house in Guessens Road, a semi, as it happens. De Soissons also built himself a house there, detached, and significantly grander than Howard's, though still comparatively modest given the kind of houses architects tend to build for themselves. I saw both these houses on my field trip to Welwyn, and frankly they both seemed a little drab.

Welwyn was always less cranky and eccentric than Letchworth, perhaps because of the sobering effect of the Great War, perhaps because it was less fully formed. For a while it was home to the Shredded Wheat factory and also briefly a minor outpost of the British film industry. The story goes that the clocking-off buzzer at the factory ruined a few takes, though I'd have thought a clocking-off buzzer was the most predictable of interruptions.

Welwyn looks even more suburban than Letchworth. The houses tend to be solid, red brick, less varied than the housing in Letchworth. The main drag here is the Parkway which runs through the centre of things, a short dual carriageway with a long grassy median between the lanes, a park you'd probably have to call it, though a very long, thin one. If you were kidnapped, blindfolded, and dumped on the Parkway, you would probably swear that you were in suburbia, though there is again a nude statue (not of Sappho) which might give you pause: you don't find them in too many suburbs.

I was walking around, looking at things, occasionally taking photographs, when I spotted a house in a little enclave of similar houses built around a small, tidy square with a central garden, just off the Parkway. The house that caught my attention was having its roof replaced: it was covered in scaffolding and the work was well under way, but I could see that the old roof tiles were being replaced with new ones that were of a wildly unmatching colour.

Knowing that conservation areas are beset with rules and regulations about the most minor changes that people are allowed to make to their houses, this sudden change and clash in roofing material colours seemed very surprising and well worth a picture or two. And as I was photographing this house and its roof, the front door of the house next door opened and a neighbour came striding out: a formidable, solid, middle-aged woman, obviously somebody not to be trifled with. I didn't want to get into an argument, though I did intend to stand my ground if she tried telling me I wasn't allowed to take pictures. But that wasn't what she had in mind at all.

She said, 'I saw you taking a picture of that roof. Isn't it *awful*? It's *completely* the wrong colour. Even when they were starting I kept saying those tiles are all wrong but they just carried on, and they said they'd blend in once they'd weathered. But I knew that couldn't be right. And anyway, finally the builder admitted that he'd ordered the wrong colour tiles and now he's going to have to take them all down and start again with the *right* colour. What a waste of time and effort. And in the meantime it just looks absolutely dreadful!'

She seemed very glad to have told me this. It may have been that she didn't want me to go away thinking her neighborhood was blighted by poor aesthetic choices, and she wanted me to know that architectural harmony would soon be restored. But I also thought it was more than that. She needed to get this off her chest, she needed to vent, and once this gush of feeling had been released she seemed much happier, much more friendly, much more serene.

For my own part, as a writer in search of local colour and anecdote, I could see this was going to make a good story, and at first I thought it was one that could be told as a comic episode about the fussiness of Hyacinth Bucket-style neighbours, but now I don't see it that way at all. Anybody with decent taste would have felt the same. Ebenezer Howard, John Ruskin, Frank Lloyd Wright, maybe even Zaha Hadid, they'd all have agreed with the woman. It wasn't about being a suburban busybody. It wasn't about disparaging the neighbours' taste. Those unmatching tiles really did look bad. The woman was absolutely right. Sometimes suburban tastes and the higher aesthetics do happen to coincide.

6

Suburban Fictions

INFIDELITY WAS A WAY OF LIFE
WITH THE SPLIT-LEVEL DWELLERS

suburban.
sin Orrie Hitt

A novel
of women who
traded husbands –
of men who
borrowed wives –
of couples who
embraced adultery
with feverish delight.

They were in a neighbourhood which looked like a toy neighbourhood taken in blocks out of a box by a child of particularly incoherent mind, and set up anyhow; here, one side of a new street; there, a large solitary public-house facing nowhere; here, another unfinished street already in ruins; there, a church; here, an immense new warehouse; there, a dilapidated old country villa; then, a medley of black ditch, sparkling cucumber-frame, rank field, richly cultivated kitchen-garden, brick viaduct, arch-spanned canal, and disorder of frowziness and fog.

As if the child had given the table a kick, and gone to sleep.

That's our mutual friend Charles Dickens writing about a fictional southwest London suburb in *Our Mutual Friend*. The most interesting part about it is that Dickens imagines the suburb as a place of childish disorder and incoherence, whereas more recent wisdom, fictional and otherwise, is that a suburb is a place of severe, regimented, stifling order, designed not by an incoherent child but by some rigid, doctrinaire architect, developer or government official. We'll come back to that.

Very early in my writing career, I had a short story broadcast on BBC radio. A journalist at the *Sheffield Star* interviewed me for a brief 'local boy makes good' article (these things are comparative). I was living in London at the time but happened to be up in Sheffield staying with my parents when the article appeared in print: by then my parents had become thoroughly convincing suburbanites.

The interviewer had asked me, reasonably enough, what my story was about and I replied, awkwardly, glibly, indeed inaccurately, 'Oh, you know, adultery in suburbia.' It was partly true but mostly not: I hadn't yet learned how to talk in public about my own writing without being embarrassed.

My mother read the article and said crossly, 'So, you're writing about adultery in suburbia, are you?' and then she didn't speak to me for the rest of the day. She was offended. She had been raised a Catholic, and she hadn't entirely lapsed. I'm sure she objected to adultery on general religious principle, but perhaps she also objected to the idea that adultery could go on in suburbia, in the very place where she now lived. And perhaps most of all she objected to, was offended by, the idea that her darling son was writing about it. The subject was, of course, never discussed again. But at least I learned that irony, about adultery or anything else, rarely works in an interview.

Of course adultery goes on in suburbia, because it goes on everywhere, and it seems a reasonable enough subject for fiction, but it's not the only thing that goes on there. I wanted to say something about novels set in suburbia, but I didn't want to write literary criticism. Who does? So I did a form of vox pop, by putting out the following message on Facebook:

Literary friends, and others, what's the best novel set in suburbia? (I will accept any definition of suburbia you choose).

I got more replies, more comments and more likes than for anything I'd ever previously posted on Facebook.

At first I wondered if there was an important distinction to be made between a novel that deals with suburbia as a *subject*, and has something to say directly about it, as opposed to a novel that 'just happens' to be set in suburbia. But in the end I think it's probably a meaningless distinction. Yes, some novels address the subject of suburbia more head on, and at greater length and in more detail than others, but by definition a novel doesn't *just happen* to be set in suburbia, or anywhere else. The novelist has decided to set it there, and by definition he or she will be saying something about it one way or another. Equally, there are a lot of novels that have just a few scenes set in suburbia and then the action moves off elsewhere, arguably somewhere more interesting. But I was happy enough to include those too.

The 'literary friends' who responded were evenly divided geographically between the United States and Britain. Obviously there is nothing remotely representative or statistically significant about these Facebook friends of mine or their opinions, but they do have a couple of positives in common – and obviously this makes them even more unrepresentative of Facebook users in general – first, they're readers, and secondly, they tend to know what they're talking about.

My question produced many supporters for what I thought of as the 'usual suspects', while also producing a considerable number of novels and novelists I'd never read or in some cases, even heard of. My notion of the usual suspects included a clutch of male American writers, above all Updike, Cheever, Roth – writers from the golden age of the late-twentieth-century American novel – also by some accounts from the golden age of American sexism and patriarchy.

None of those three writers had a simple relationship with the suburbs, but Updike's strikes me as the healthiest and most interesting, perhaps because he wasn't much of a suburbanite. Rabbit Angstrom, the protagonist of Updike's *Rabbit* novels, the owner of a Toyota dealership in New Jersey, was a satisfyingly long way from the 'real' Updike. There's no possibility of thinking of him as Updike's alter ego, which is perhaps why Updike stuck with him for four decades, treating him without mockery or condescension, as he lived a thoroughly American suburban life, with all its pleasures as well as its agonies.

John Cheever is, apparently, sometimes known as the Chekhov of suburbia, though not by anybody I've ever met, and the general wisdom is that he depicts the American East Coast suburbs as places of wearying routine, banality, anxiety, ambivalence, with too much booze, and widespread sexual frustrations that are not resolved by actually having sex. As ever, these don't strike me as by any means uniquely suburban problems, but yes that's the milieu he writes about, and he's not exactly a cheerleader for the suburban way of life. His short story 'The Swimmer' (1964) still seems to me his masterpiece and although it certainly takes place in a wealthy suburbia of swimming pools and too much gin, it contains a large amount of fantasy, and the loneliness, the bleakness, the impending sense of darkness and mortality, seem universal rather than suburban.

I'm never sure how significant it is that Cheever once rented the house in Ossining, Connecticut, where fellow novelist Richard Yates had previously lived. Yates's *Revolutionary Road* (1961) certainly had supporters on my Facebook feed. The plot of the novel involves a suburban couple, the Wheelers, who are desperate to prove they're not totally suburban. They plan to move to Paris, though for one reason and another they don't. This strikes me as far more Chekhovian than most of Cheever.

When it comes to Philip Roth, there are particular suburban anxieties that centre around his and his characters' Jewishness, anxieties that some of his critics have decided make him a self-hating Jew. This is not an argument that a Gentile should get too deeply involved in, but it seems to me that Roth wrote, satirically, but not without affection, about Jewish immigrants who had moved up, very rapidly, from the ghetto to the suburbs, where they were leading prosperous all-American lives. *Goodbye Columbus,* first published in *Paris Review* in 1959, strikes me as the touchstone here.

The fact that Roth had an eye for the absurdity and vulgarity of suburban life and its materialism, doesn't seem, to me, to make him a monster, rather it's what made him a novelist. Other views are possible. Irving Howe denounced Roth, in an essay titled 'Roth Reconsidered' in *Commentary* magazine, in these terms:

> there is a parasitic relation to the embattled sentiments and postures of older Jewish writers in America – though without any recognition that, by now, simply to launch attacks on middle-class suburbia is to put oneself at the head of the suburban parade, just as to mock the uprightness of immigrant Jews is to become the darling of their 'liberated' suburban children.

When this was written in 1972 Roth was thirty-nine (and Howe was fifty-two), so Roth may well have been considered an 'older writer' by some, most probably by those liberated suburban children – the 'never trust anybody over thirty' contingent – but quite how this would make him their darling remains unclear.

Joseph Heller's *Something Happened* (1974) – written when Heller was in his mid-forties – was championed on my Facebook feed by the novelist Bruce Bauman who wrote, 'Everyone wanted Heller to write *Catch 23*, most of them missing the tragedy behind the human comedy. *Something Happened* is the great tragic-comic take-down of Manhattan corporate life, suburbia – America without a soul. It's pure genius.'

Some of the American outliers that popped up included Don DeLillo's *White Noise*, Thomas Berger's *Neighbors,* even Nabokov's *Lolita.* One or two people wondered whether Cormac McCarthy's *The Road* counts as suburban fiction since it's set in a post-apocalyptic world, but the general feeling was, yes, it counts. And I was delighted to see that somebody was cheering for H.G. Wells's *War of the Worlds.*

The novelist Steve Erickson suggested *The Man Whose Teeth Were All Exactly Alike* by Philip K. Dick, which I assumed was science fiction but isn't. Erickson wrote,

> Not SF, Geoff, in that everything that happens in it conforms to what is & was real and possible, albeit unlikely. This is from Dick's strange West Coast suburban period that no one would publish until after he was dead and which remains infuriatingly overlooked, particularly by the same literary establishment that had to be browbeaten in the first place into recognizing the SF work. These suburban novels include not only *Teeth* but *Confessions of a Crap Artist,* and *In Milton Lumky Territory*, all three of which I would easily put on any list of Dick's 12 greatest novels. (To their credit, the Brits published them first.)

If all these selections and recommendations sound thoroughly 'male', and I accept that they do, it's worth saying that as many women as men advocated works by male novelists. And interestingly, there was far less consensus when it came to novels written by women. The nominations included *Patchwork Planet* and *Amateur Marriage* by Anne Tyler, *Where'd You Go, Bernadette?* by Maria Semple, *Mrs. Caliban* by Rachel Ingalls, and Emily St John Mandel's *Lola Quartet*, much of which is set in suburban Florida.

Donna's Tartt's *The Goldfinch* (2014), which I had read and liked very much, was recommended for its fabulous description of a suburb outside Las Vegas that is being abandoned and falling into decay even as it's being built, though the work as a whole is a long way from being a suburban novel, it seems to me. Something very similar might be said about Gillian Flynn's *Gone Girl* (2012), in which a married couple move to a rented house by the Mississippi River. The narrator here is the husband,

> ... a house that screams Suburban Nouveau Riche, the kind of place I aspired to as a kid from my split-level shag-carpet side of town. The kind of house that is immediately familiar: a geometrically grand, unchallenging, new, new, new house that my wife would – and did – detest.
>
> 'Should I remove my soul before I come inside?' Her first line upon arrival.

Later in the book we discover that she has no soul to remove.

I was glad somebody suggested Sylvia Plath's *The Bell Jar*, worth inclusion for this passage alone,

> I stepped from the air-conditioned compartment on to the station platform, and the motherly breath of the

suburbs enfolded me. It smelt of lawn sprinklers and station wagons and tennis rackets and dogs and babies.

A summer calm laid its soothing hand over everything, like death.

I love that swerve, the way the language and the thought seems to be heading one way, then suddenly goes another. It also leaves me wondering what lawn sprinklers smell like.

My British Facebookers came up with a very different, more scattered, selection of novels and novelists. I thought somebody would be rooting for Charles Dickens, as above, but nobody was. The ones they went for included the novels of Barbara Pym, Philip Hensher's Sheffield novels, *The Cement Garden* by Ian McEwan, Julian Barnes's *Metroland*, *The Rotter's Club* by Jonathan Coe, *Beyond Black* by Hilary Mantel.

One early contender was *The Diary of a Nobody* (1888–92) by George and Weedon Grossmith – I suspect few readers in the United States have even heard of it – but I'd recently reread it as research. The Pooters, mother, father, son, live in Holloway in Brickfield Lane (a brickfield being a sure sign that development and suburban expansion are going on), and if we can trust the original illustrations, they are renting a substantial though not at all palatial end of terrace house.

It's certainly suburbia but the Pooters have a servant, and they drink champagne, even as they know it's not the best kind. Pooter is, I suppose, a classic comic everyman, prickly, pompous, much concerned with social position, sensitive to slights, untroubled by self-knowledge or a sense of humour, and there are certainly times rereading *The Diary of a Nobody* when I felt I was having my own sense of humour failure. I mean, even that name Pooter – is that a good joke? Pooter also has two friends, one a vulgarian, one a bore, named Cumming and Gowing; does even that really qualify as humour? And as for a character named Murray Posh …

Of course all this is subjective, some readers are no doubt laughing like drains both with and at Pooter. Inevitably we are inclined to think we're superior to Pooter: we see him in a way that he can't see himself, and a moment comes towards the end of the book, with the appearance of an American named Hardfur Huttle (I know), when the text starts to become self-referential.

Over dinner Huttle says,

Do you know 'happy medium' are two words which mean 'incredible mediocrity'? … The happy medium is no more or less than a vulgar half measure. A man who loves champagne and finding a pint too little, fears to face a whole bottle and has recourse to an imperial pint, will never build a Brooklyn Bridge or an Eiffel Tower. No, he is half-hearted, he is a half-measure – respectable – in fact a happy medium, and will spend the rest of his days in a suburban villa with a stucco-column portico, resembling a four-post bed.

Pooter does, in some sense, take this on board. He finds that Huttle's attitudes remind him of his own son, named Lupin (I know, I *know)* who a few pages later moves out of the family home for a furnished apartment in Bayswater. Pooter says that Holloway has always been good enough for him, and Lupin replies, 'It is no question of being good or bad. There is no money in it, and I am not going to rot away my life in the suburbs.'

It's possible to see Lupin as a soul brother of Karim, the biracial, bisexual teenage narrator of Hanif Kureishi's quasi-autobiographical novel *The Buddha of Suburbia* (1993), a great title that doesn't quite fit the story it tells. The titular 'Buddha' is Haroon Amir, the narrator's father, an Indian Muslim from Bombay, now a civil servant settled in Bromley. Dad becomes an exotic dispenser of wisdom to his suburban neighbours, but it's not specifically Buddhist wisdom, so he's not so much a Buddha as an all-purpose guru.

Some of Karim's complaints against his father are standard-issue. He wonders why his father 'condemned his own son to a dreary London suburb', and he offers the opinion that 'in the suburbs people rarely dreamed of striking out for happiness', even though the novel is full of people who do exactly that, and a surprising number of them stop dreaming and actually *do* strike out.

There is one very surprising and telling sentence in the novel, about a character named Eva, a quasi-Bohemian interior designer, the woman Haroon moves in with, having deserted the family home, though not entirely deserted his family. Karim says of her, 'I saw she wanted to scour that suburban stigma right off her body. She didn't realise it was in the blood and not on the skin; she didn't see there could be nothing more suburban than suburbanites repudiating themselves.'

Personally I think this is profoundly true, and since this scouring is what Kureishi's narrator metaphorically also does for most of the book, I'd like to think there was some overarching irony in the novel, but I'm not sure that there is. I think Kureishi and his creation just really hate the suburbs, and that's that.

Two writers kept popping up that I'm just a little ashamed to say I'd never read: Zadie Smith and Barbara Pym. Smith's *White Teeth* (2000) has many admirers, though there's evidence that Zadie Smith is no longer one of them. It happens with novelists and their first novels, especially one like this which is so crammed to bursting point with *stuff*. It is, in a couple of senses, all over the place: in Bulgaria in World War II, in Bengal for the Indian Mutiny in 1857, in Kingston, Jamaica for the 1907 earthquake, in Birmingham for a burning of *The Satanic Verses*.* But it's essentially rooted in Willesden, a suburb of northwest London,

---

* Salman Rushdie is quoted on my paperback copy of *White Teeth* as saying, 'I was delighted.'

which on the evidence of the book, is a place of staggering diversity, a crucible of interracial sex, Muslim fundamentalism, Australian squatters, animal-rights activists, millennial Jehovah's Witnesses, and at least one Jewish scientist who is playing god with the genes of mice.

Some of the characters think Willesden is a 'nice' place though it's not clear that the author feels that way. Clara (of West Indian heritage) is married to Archie (white, English). The novel tells us, 'She did not love Archie, but had made up her mind … to devote herself to him if he would take her away. And now he had; and though it wasn't Morocco or Belgium or Italy, it was nice – not the promised land – but nice, nicer than anywhere she had ever been.' And there's Alsana married to Samad, both Bangladeshi, she's a seamstress making fetish outfits, he's an overqualified waiter in an 'Indian' restaurant. Alsana thinks, 'Willesden was not as pretty as Queens Park, but it was nice, no denying it.'

There are some good jokes in the book about the naivety of youthful suburban attempts at sophistication. A member of the Keepers of the Eternal and Victorious Islamic Nation (acronym KEVIN) introduces one of the fellow members, Sister Aeyisha, by saying, 'She's an African goddess.'

'Really?' said Millat, impressed. 'Whereabouts you from?'

'Clapham North,' said Sister Aeyisha with a shy smile.

Millat is a charismatic local bad boy, 'He was so big in Cricklewood, in Willesden, in West Hampstead, the summer of 1990, that nothing he did later in his life could top it.' We all know the type.

I admit I did find it a bit disappointing that many of the book's threads finally come together not in Willesden or any other suburb, but in Trafalgar Square, as though ordinary life may happen in the suburbs, but drama, intensity, *denouements* can only happen in the very centre of London.

I find it fun to imagine a meeting between Zadie Smith and Barbara Pym, two very different writers, but not quite as different as you might think. They were in fact alive at the same time, but only just: Smith was born in 1975, Pym died in 1980, so a meeting of minds would require some time travel, but if that were possible, I think they'd find they had plenty in common. They were both Oxbridge women – Smith at Cambridge, Pym at Oxford, both studied English, and both in their different ways, at different times, lived in and wrote about the suburbs: Smith had Willesden, Pym had Barnes. Pym lived in Nassau Road, and her neighbour, briefly, was Paul Raymond, he of the porn mag and strip club empire.

Smith and Pym are both at times very funny writers, though Pym's wit is much dryer. The opening line of *No Fond Return of Love* (1961), which I find hilarious, seems designed to deter a whole swathe of readers. 'There are various ways of mending a broken heart, but perhaps going to a learned conference is one of the more unusual.' No 'perhaps' about it, I'd say. And when you discover that the book is set in the milieu of female literary indexers, well, you probably have a pretty shrewd idea of whether or not this book's for you.

No Fond Return of Love is Pym's great suburban novel. The central character, Dulcie Mainwaring, 'halfway to being a spin-ster', is one of the indexers, living in what was her mother's large suburban house in an unnamed London suburb, but Barnes certainly fits the bill. 'Dulcie lived in a pleasant part of London which, while it was, undoubtedly a suburb, was "highly desirable" and, to continue in the estate agent's words, "took the overflow from Kensington". "And Harrods *do* deliver" as her next door neighbour Mrs. Beltane so often repeated.'

Barnes is clearly a suburban cut above Willesden, but still sneered at by those who live closer to central London. Dulcie occasionally rents out rooms in her house, not from economic necessity, though it's clearly not a place anybody actually wants to live. Most fellow Londoners find it hard to get there. One of her lodgers, her niece Laurel, goes there by taxi and observes,

'Olympia had seemed the last bulwark of civilisation. And then when they came to the suburban roads, with people doing things in gardens, she had wanted to tap on the glass and tell the driver to turn back.' Aylwin Forbes, the book's main love interest, a poetry scholar deplores 'the stultifying oppression of the suburbs,' though Forbes turns out to have unexpectedly humble origins.

At the end of the book, a newly married couple move to Neasden. This is regarded as a social, economic and perhaps moral, failure. For readers of certain, perhaps several, generations Neasden is best known as the nondescript no man's land mocked by *Private Eye* magazine. It turns out that Pym's novel was published the year *Private Eye* was founded, so perhaps there was something in the air at the time about the awfulness of Neasden, though *Private Eye* was printed in Neasden, so that may be the cause as far as they were concerned. Neasden was described by Betjeman as 'a place of gnomes and ordinary people', which may or may not be an insult.* It was also, at one time, famous as the home of Twiggy.

Despite Aylwin Forbes identifying the stultifying oppression of Barnes, there's no shortage of desire in Barbara Pym's version of the suburb, though there is, apparently, very little sex, and very little mixing of the races. The nearest we come to exoticism, or what we'd now call diversity, is Senhor MacBride-Pereira a Brazilian diplomat who lives in an upper-storey flat next door to Dulcie and spends a lot of time looking out of his window observing the comings and goings of his neighbours and not quite understanding what he sees.

The truth is, to a considerable extent he's seeing suburban mating rituals, and evidence of suburban passions. These passions are not in themselves repressed, but they're expressed with

---

* My paperback copy of *No Fond Return of Love* comes with an approving quotation from Betjeman about Barbara Pym being 'A splendid humorous writer,' which seems rather to miss the point.

great reticence. In the end, in Pym's novel, everybody seems to get some of what they want, at least some of the time. That's not exactly the usual subject of 'great literature' – it's not the 'message' of *Moby Dick* or *Naked Lunch* – but it sounds very much like what most people settle for in life, and not only in the suburbs.

The one writer suggested by men and women, British and American, was (perhaps inevitably) J.G. Ballard, especially *The Unlimited Dream Company* (1979), *Kingdom Come* (2006), and *Running Wild* (1988). Ballard, whom I used to know slightly, is the poster boy for suburban ambivalence and has in various interviews described his love and hate of the suburbs. In an interview that appeared in *Re/Search* magazine in 1984 he said,

> Everywhere – all over Africa and South America … you see these suburbs springing up. They represent the opti-mum of what people want. There's a certain sort of logic leading towards these immaculate suburbs. And they're terrifying, because they are the *death of the soul … This* is the prison this planet is being turned into.' [But in that same interview he says] 'Suburbia is the cutting-edge of social change. The people here are comfortable and well-off enough to be able to explore different pastimes and hobbies, and to experiment with different lifestyles. Everything started here – from the fitness crusade to wife-swapping. Hi-fi systems and VCRs enabled people, for the first time, to choose their own music, and not have it dictated to by a metropolitan elite who decide what goes on the radio, or into concert halls or art galleries.

He gave a somewhat different account in an interview with the *Guardian* in 2008:

I came to live in Shepperton in 1960. I thought: the future isn't in the metropolitan areas of London. I want to go out to the new suburbs, near the film studios. This was the England I wanted to write about, because this was the new world that was emerging.

So which is it? Are the suburbs an emerging new world, the cutting edge of social change or a place where the soul dies? Are they places where we feel safe? Safe enough for us to indulge violent fantasies? Or are they places where we're constantly fearing that those fantasies might come true? Perhaps they can be all these things simultaneously, and at the very least the suburbs provided Ballard with most of his best material.

Mike Bonsall's two magnificently obsessive Ballard online concordances, one of Ballard's own written works, one of his interviews, cite literally hundreds of Ballard's uses of the words suburb, suburbs, suburbia, along with much less frequent usages of suburbanites, suburbanised, suburbanising, suburbanisation, and one usage of a word I've never come across anywhere else – 'suburbed'.

A prime example of the Ballardian high style, is the opening of *Kingdom Come*, his last novel, published in 2006, set in Brooklands in Surrey; 'The suburbs dream of violence. Asleep in their drowsy villas, sheltered by benevolent shopping malls, they wait patiently for the nightmares that will take them into a more passionate world …' I think we're entitled to ask whether it's the suburbs that dream of violence (can suburbs dream?), or Ballard's narrator, the other characters in the novel, or Ballard himself, and of course it may be all of these, but Ballard's personal history would have given him plenty of reasons to have violent dreams.

He was born in 1930 in Shanghai, where his parents lived in Amherst Avenue about 800 yards outside the International Settlement, an enclave for expat businessmen, which in extant photographs looks like a transplanted, upscale Anglo-American suburb. His life changed completely when the Japanese invaded Shanghai in 1943, and the Ballard family was shipped off to the Lunghua Civilian Assembly Centre, an internment camp, where they spent the rest of the war; this was the real-life experience that fed into his non-suburban novel *Empire of the Sun* (1984).

Having survived such an experience, anybody might be inclined to spend the rest of their days living quietly in the suburbs, which is what Ballard did in some sense, in that after the sudden, unexpected, early death of his wife, he was left as a single parent raising three children in a suburban semi in Shepperton. To be absolutely correct, Shepperton is officially a town rather than a suburb, but Ballard himself usually, though not always, referred to it as a suburb.

Day-to-day life may have been thoroughly domestic and mundane, but once at his writing desk, Ballard allowed his imagination to invent scenarios of violent suburban disaster. He knew better than most that terrible things can happen anywhere, not least in suburbia. Yes, the suburbs may, by many accounts, be superficially uneventful and orderly, but when it comes to creating a plot, the basic dynamics of fictional narrative demand that something must happen, and wherever there's order, there must soon be disorder. What comes after that is up for grabs. Ballard's angle, his unique selling point, was to write about characters who embraced whatever disaster befell them, and ultimately thrived on it.

Like many writers of a certain generation, I made the obligatory pilgrimage down to Shepperton to gaze at the outside of Ballard's semi. It was right after his death, and before the house was sold. Ballard's car was still sitting in the driveway. It seemed a nice enough, unexceptional house, pricey no doubt since it was within easy walking distance of the station, equally close to a couple of pubs and to the local golf course. There's a line by Michael Bracewell in *England is Mine* (2009) in which he denounces the suburbs

for their 'colonisation in the name of golf, God and gardening'.
I think we can safely say that Ballard did not embrace God, and
looking at the plain patch of untended lawn in front of his house,
he definitely didn't embrace gardening, and I do so hope he didn't
embrace golf, though I have no absolute proof of that.

  Ballard's most extreme, and downright dodgy, depiction of
suburban sexual transgression occurs in *The Unlimited Dream
Company* (1979), set in Shepperton, or at least in an imagined
version of the place. The central character, Blake, arrives there
having stolen a light aircraft and crashed it into the Thames. He
then finds himself unable to leave.

> I knew then that I would stay in this small town until
> I had mated with everyone there – the women, men and
> children, their dogs and cats, the cage-birds in the front
> parlours, the cattle in the water-meadow, the deer in the
> park, the flies in this bedroom – and fused us together
> into a new being.

It sounds as exhausting as it does illegal, but Ballard, of course,
was not a literalist.

  Perhaps he's buying into an extreme form of the notion that
life in the suburbs is so stultifying that people need to engage in
wild and transgressive sex in order to feel alive, in order to feel
anything. It was an idea common in American pulp novels of
the 1960s. By that point in history all kinds of people, not least
the suburban ones, were feeling 'liberated' or 'permissive', and
were 'experimenting' with sex, though I suspect these suburban
pulp novels were mostly read by an audience who felt they were
missing out on the fun.

  A not quite random sampling of these books includes
Suburban Sin by Orrie Hitt, one of the most productive of all
pulp writers. He was also the author of *Suburban Wife*, and
Sexurbia County – a nod to Edmund Wilson. There's *Suburbia*

After Dark by Carlyon Gibbs 'restless women who make themselves more available than younger girls – to any boy with nerve!' There's *Daytime in Suburbia* by Susanna West, 'Young housewives, made vulnerable by boredom and neglect, forgetting marital vows and morality in a desperate search for excitement and fulfilment.'

There's *Swapping in Suburbia* by Herb Muller,

> The exclusive suburb of Westown is invaded by two creatures of evil, posing as art experts – Gary Mireau and his nymph-like protégé who poses as his niece, Katherine. The plan? To arrange sex parties, then film the orgiastic activities with a secretly placed camera. The film is then used for blackmail purposes if the 'performers' prove difficult. But Gary did not reckon with Westown's own bizarre activities …

It's not quite Ballardian but it's not too far away. The fact that this in no way resembles any suburbia that anybody has ever lived in, is of course a big part of the attraction.

There was some non-heterosexual pulp too, and I did find one lesbian-themed novel by Marjorie Lee titled *The Lion House* and described in its blurb as 'the novel that rocked suburbia', but as far as I can tell the mention of suburbia in a book title caused far less of a frisson in the gay community than it did in the straight.

There is even, and I only found this recently, a book titled *Adultery in Suburbia* by Matthew Bradley, published by Gold Star Books in 1964. The blurb tells us, 'Her illness was nymphomania, but there were others in town far more disturbed.'

I read the book thoroughly in the interests of research, and it is, I think you'd have to say, a strange one. A couple, Bill and Sandra Gale, arrive in Columbus, Ohio from Los Angeles. He works in insurance and has been transferred after some trouble back in California involving his wife's activities there. These aren't

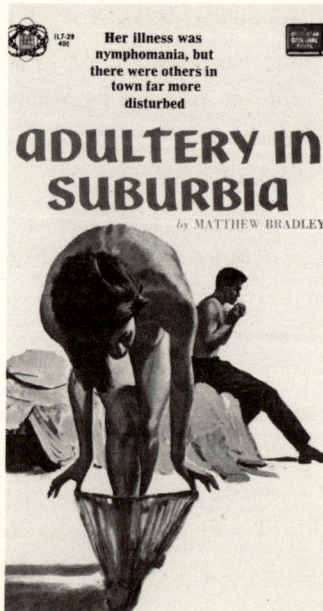

described in any detail, but since Sandra is the nymphomaniac of the blurb it's easy to join the dots.

They move into a tiny suburban enclave of just four houses, which are not described in any detail, though we learn there's a shared swimming pool and a communal barbecue area. The inhabitants call themselves the Cliffdwellers, and they throw a cocktail party to welcome their new neighbours. This has never happened to me in suburbia. Bill is very happy with the move to Ohio. 'Here all was different. Even the grass smelled good. And the neighbors, he thought gratefully, were real people. None of this sick oversexed Hollywood stuff out here.' Sandra is less enamoured.

Things move comparatively slowly. Sandra struggles with her condition, but has only limited success; she develops a phantom pregnancy and becomes utterly insane, although her ultimate fate remains unclear, at least to me. This is all treated rather more seriously than I imagine the pulp market would have needed or wanted. Fortunately lurid prose breaks out from time to time: 'Nell smiled evilly and spat in his face. "No bedroom, buster. You want it, take it. Right here on the kitchen floor like the pig you are."' He takes it.

But then there's another issue … 'the Cliffdwellers were suddenly hit with something more insidious than Sandra's nymphomania. *Eminent domain.* That's the American equivalent of a compulsory purchase order. The county wants to widen the local highway, and that will required the demolition of the four houses belonging to the Cliffdwellers. They fight the power, largely on the grounds that the county is paying them less than their properties are worth; but they lose.

> In March, the bulldozers and the earth-moving equipment came to River Road to widen it into a bad mockery of a Los Angeles freeway. And where Number 12, 14, 16 and 18 had once stood, with a pool and a barbecue between them, with lush lawns and fragrant shrubbery, there was only an ugly shape of red clay. And the late rains came down, and the cars, unseeing, uncaring, hissed past on the highway that didn't really need widening.

Elegiac? Yes, indeed. Pulp? Well yes, but the writing is better than it needs to be. My mother would have had a fit over that title, and certainly about some of the goings on described, but I don't think she'd have considered it absolute filth. I wonder how Matthew Bradley's mother felt.

7

The Suburban Garden

If we think of the suburbs as an interzone between the country and the city, and as we've seen, historically many have, then the suburban population will be made up of rural folk moving closer to the city, and urban folk moving farther away. Of course, in current circumstances, there will be many more in the latter group than in the former, but the attitude new suburban dwellers have towards gardens and gardening will depend to a large extent on the direction they're coming from.

If you arrive from the country you might regard the garden as a very small agricultural plot, a place to grow food, a place where you work the land and the land works for you. But if you arrive from the city, you may well never have had a garden before, you're unlikely to have any gardening skills, you might not even be able to tell a weed from a flower, but one way or another you're going to have to deal with this new outdoor space. You could call in a professional, but unless you're seriously enfeebled, we in the suburbs regard that as cheating. Or you could do nothing at all and call it rewilding, but in suburbia this will fool nobody.

You may feel that you have the low-level skills to take care of the lawn: that domesticated, miniaturised, suburbanised version of the field, the meadow, the village green, although experts will tell you there's nothing simple about lawn care. Equally you may learn that the lawn isn't as simple and innocent as it first appears – see Joni Mitchell's *The Hissing of Summer Lawns,* Richard Brautigan's *The Revenge of the Lawn,* or Stephen King's *Lawnmower Man* – but this may not worry you at first: you buy a lawnmower and away you go.

Beyond that however, chances are you're going to need some advice. Today you can you obtain gardening wisdom from any number of TV pundits, few if any of whom would consider themselves suburban. Before that there was radio. The first person to broadcast gardening advice on the radio, in 1923, was Marion Cran, who'd had a bestseller with *The Garden of Ignorance* (1913) and later wrote *The Story of My Ruin* (1924) and *The Joy of the Ground* (1928); she didn't make a career as a broadcaster but she obviously had a great gift for book titles.

But the dispensing of gardening advice started long before that. There is a book titled *The Suburban Gardener and Villa Companion*, by J.C. Loudon, first published in 1838. The author ranks gardens and homes from first rate to fourth rate, and his notion of a suburb is not wholly like yours and mine. He writes, 'As the characteristics of the first class are a paddock and dairy, so those of a suburban residence of the first class are a park and a farm; and the extent of the whole of such a residence can scarcely be less than from 50 to 100 acres.' This seems to be describing the suburban gardens on another planet, but later he moves down the scale and writes, 'The suburbs of towns are alone calculated to afford a maximum of comfort and enjoyment at a minimum of expense,' which seems as true now as then: you get more for your money outside the big cities. There's a BBC documentary by Michael Collins, titled *Everyday Eden, A Potted History of the Suburban Garden*, which suggests that many people, mostly older people inevitably, move out of London and go to the suburbs precisely so they can have a garden.

In *Gardens for Town and Suburb* by V.N. Solly, published in 1926, the author draws a distinction between front and back gardens. He writes, 'It seems right that the front garden should suggest an open if not effusive friendliness, rather than the greater reticence and mystery which is allowed in the country.' Personally I see a great deal of reticence in people's suburban front gardens, though only a limited amount of mystery. I think that, as a rule, a front garden is for others, whereas a back garden is for yourself. Solly also says, 'Unfortunately a trend of hysteria seems to possess the pioneers of a newly developed suburb. Neither of the town nor of the country, they have no tradition, though many strange manifestations both of building and garden arrangement may arise from a real enthusiasm and interest in the undertaking.' And he concludes, 'The suburban garden may be restricted in size, but it is much freer from other considerations on gardening ambition which are felt in the town.' It's not absolutely clear if he approves of this freedom and ambition, but obviously he doesn't approve at all of hysteria.

Sometimes suburbanites have advice forced upon them. The tenants of the Becontree estate in Dagenham, in its time the largest subsidised housing estate in the world, received a handbook telling them how to behave in and around their new home. This included advice about how to care for their gardens, and to be fair, many of the new inhabitants came from the slums of the East End and probably had little or no experience of gardening. Even so, the advice in the 1933 handbook seems a little snooty, 'Neglect of the Garden spoils the appearance of any house …

the front garden should be neat and tidy throughout the year.' This must have been a hard rule to enforce, but substantial prizes were given to the best-kept gardens, initial nominations coming from the local rent collectors.

Not all advice has to be heeded and not all gardening books or programmes have to be instructional. Some are just for wallowing in. My favourite in this category, first a gloriously quirky TV documentary, then a tie-in book, is *The Front Garden* by Candida Lycett Green and Christopher Sykes, first transmitted on Christmas Day 1979, and subsequently much repeated. You expect it to be a quaint period piece, but it's far more interesting than that.

Lycett Green was the daughter of John Betjeman, and the book is dedicated to him. Lycett Green writes in the introduction, 'England is thick with wonderful gardens' and she says that the gardeners she talked to, 'were extremely contented people, more often than not in their sixties, seventies and eighties, and to say that the best gardens were created through love and happiness might sound corny, but it was my indisputable conclusion.' It's conspicuously true that gardening is not a young person's game. There are few, if any, teenagers out there saying, 'I *hate* you, Dad, because you won't let me plant a mulberry tree.'

Lycett Green's film and book are not only about suburban gardens, but the ones that stand out for me are those where a grand scheme or ambition has expressed itself through suburban limitations: garden railways, model cathedrals, layouts as formal as Versailles but in a plot half the size of a tennis court. Take for example one Mr Colquohoun, owner of an extremely orderly garden in Stickney, Lincolnshire, a garden without a curved line in the place. Mr Colquohoun was once an engineer, and is quoted as saying, 'Orderliness in the home I think is extended into the garden and the majority of people enjoy it. There are the odd ones who say they don't like that sort of thing, they like everything in a turmoil and an uproar. I'm afraid we don't belong to that school.'

There's a fair bit of topiary in *The Front Garden*: a giant pheasant in a garden in Wickhambrook, in Suffolk, privet clipped into spheres and trained around wire forms to create geometrical shapes, in Mr Gregg's garden in Kidlington, Oxfordshire. And maybe topiary is as orderly as a suburban garden can get. Perhaps it's also as *suburban* as a garden can get. It hasn't always been that way, although there have always been some doubts about topiary's essential aesthetic merit.

Topiary is an ancient art. Pliny, writing in the first century AD describes 'cypress trees cut into tableaux of *opus topiarium*, hunt-scenes, fleets of ships, and all sorts of image', although Pliny here is using the term *opus topiarium* to refer to the entire work of ornamental garden design.

Topiary was popular in early Renaissance Italy, although Sir Francis Bacon in 'Of Gardens' (1625) had his reservations. He wrote,

> For the ordering of the ground within the great hedge, I leave it to variety of device; advising nevertheless, that whatsoever form you cast it into, first it be not too busy, or full of work; wherein I, for my part, do not like images cut out in juniper or other garden stuff; they be for children. Little low hedges round, like welts, with some pretty pyramids, I like well; and in some places fair columns, upon frames of carpenter's work.

The 1986 edition of *The Oxford Companion to Gardens* tells us that 'the more frivolous species of topiary sculpture continued through the seventeenth century and into the eighteenth but became increasingly the province of parvenu tradesmen.' I suppose 'parvenu tradesmen' isn't quite synonymous with 'dreadful suburbanites' but it's a sign that topiary has often been associated with those who supposedly lacked taste. This strikes me as unfair and untrue.

The best-known contemporary topiarist I'm aware of goes by the name of Hedgecutter Man. His real name is Tim Bushe: does anybody doubt that names are destiny? In his primary profession he was an architect, and he drifted accidentally into his current career, or hobby, making topiary for domestic gardens in North London, and he gives the money to charity, currently to Extinction Rebellion. He's a natural, with an art-school training, who doesn't take his work too seriously, and although he's cut hedges into trains, a cannon and a Henry Moore-style reclining nude, he specialises in animals: cats, owls, and most famously a parade of elephants in Romilly Road, Finsbury Park, London.

When I went to see those elephants, it did worry me that they were ominously near to the Arsenal football ground, however the word on the street is that passing fans are appreciative and respectful. But there are other worries. A neighbour tried to cut down the elephants on the grounds that they shielded the transactions of drug dealers who lived in the basement flat behind the hedge. The tenants had been housed by Islington's Partners For Improvement, and according to newspaper reports the flat was raided by police in 2018 and the inhabitants accused of smoking crack and worshipping Satan, which does seem at odds with the otherwise apparently quiet suburban street. The concerned neighbour was prevented from his act of topiary destruction by other neighbours, and Mr Bushe, who is obviously a man of some wit said, 'I don't think napalming the garden and hedges is the answer. If you had someone occupying and looking after the flat downstairs it wouldn't be happening. PFI needs to get someone in and make sure it's not a crack dealer.' Sounds too simple, doesn't it?

One night, shortly after I went to see the elephants, there was a street race in which a driver lost control of his car and smacked into the garden wall in front of the topiary elephants, which would surely have come as quite a disturbance if you were in the basement flat quietly smoking crack and worshipping Satan. The wall was partly demolished and the elephants were damaged, but not irretrievably. Both wall and topiary were restored, with the elephants being given supporting frames, and they were expected to make a full recovery. However, word recently came through that half the herd has been lost to honey fungus.

Topiary, then, may be redeemable as an amusing or skilfull feature of the suburban garden. But there's one element that so far hasn't been, and probably can't be, redeemed, and that's the garden gnome. The fact that former prime minister John Major had a father and a brother who had been in the gnome manufacturing business, did nothing for his political gravitas, and even less for the gravitas of the gnome.

Gnomes may seem tasteless, naff, ugly, at best kitsch, and laughable in all the wrong ways, but they're still very much with us. As I wander around and peer over fences into people's gardens, I see them all the time, in various shapes and sizes, made of concrete or terracotta or plastic, some quite crude, some very well made. Most often the gnomes are just standing there, occasionally fishing or pushing a wheelbarrow, once in a great while doing something risqué like showing their buttocks; and it's apparent that many people absolutely love them, just as much as, and possibly more than, some other people absolutely hate them. Maybe some of this displaying of gnomes is ironic, or a joke, or maybe it's to show that the inhabitants don't care about the opinions of others. Whatever the reason, there they are, in quantity.

The word gnome or genomos or gnomus was coined by the fifteenth-century alchemist and physician Paracelsus in his *Liber de Nymphis, sylphis, pygmaeis et salamandris et de caeteris spiritibus*. But he didn't invent the gnome *per se*. They seem to have been part of folklore – earth spirits, guardians of the world's natural resources – so it seems reasonable enough to have one protecting your garden, suburban or otherwise.

Alexander Pope introduced the word to the English language in 'The Rape of the Lock' but it was evidently a word that needed explaining to his readers. In the poem's dedication to Mrs

Arabella Fermor, Pope attributes the term to the Rosicrucians and cites his source as

> a French book call'd 'Le Comte de Gabalis,' which both in its title and size is so like a Novel, that many of the Fair Sex have read it for one by mistake. According to these Gentlemen, the four Elements are inhabited by Spirits, which they call Sylphs, Gnomes, Nymphs, and Salamanders. The Gnomes or Daemons of Earth delight in mischief.

Pope's gnomes do bear some relation to those of Paracelsus, but very little to those of the suburban garden. For one thing, they can fly:

> The Gnome rejoicing bears her gifts away,
> Spreads his black wings, and slowly mounts to day.

I think having a gnome with black wings sitting in the garden would be very eye-catching but I've yet to see one.

The first decorative garden gnomes were manufactured in Germany in the middle of the eighteenth century, although garden statues and figurines of dwarves and earth spirits had been around in formal gardens since at least the Renaissance. The kind of gnomes we're familiar with were introduced to England in the mid-nineteenth century by Sir Charles Isham who installed a hundred of them in the grounds of his home at Lamport Hall, Northamptonshire. It's fair to say this was not a suburban garden, and his daughter subsequently had all but one of the gnomes removed in the interests of 'good taste'.

In 1934 the Blackgang Chine Gardens, a tourist attraction on the Isle of Wight, introduced a Gnome Garden. The garden's owner and creator, Bruce Dabell, said it was 'a reflection of the garden fashions in suburbia'. This sounds like a sneer as much as a gesture of approval. The place is now the Blackgang Chine Land of Imagination. The gnome garden has gone though there is now a Valley of Dodos and a Rumpus Lawn.

The Royal Horticultural Society takes a sniffy view of gnomes. Gnomes were banned from the Chelsea Flower Show for the first hundred years of its existence. There was a one-year dispensation for the centenary in 2013 and then the ban went back into place. There have been occasional, and no doubt ironic, protests about these exclusions, and people have turned up at the show dressed as gnomes. There are also a number of gnome liberation movements, designed to 'free' garden gnomes, chiefly by stealing them. Such a stolen gnome forms part of the plot of the movie *Amélie* (2001), which was massively popular around the world, though I don't think it led to any great universal love of gnomes. Their status as an emblem of suburbia may be a large part of the problem.

I did once own a gnome modelled on Arnold Schwarzenegger's Terminator (the Gnominator), but I didn't have it in the garden. And If you need some sense of just how irredeemable garden gnomes are, consider that Terry Scott was once one of the eponymous leads in *The Gnomes of Dulwich* (1969), a lost sitcom of which only the stills remains. I don't believe that anybody's grieving.

I was in Manchester. It wasn't strictly speaking a field trip to the suburbs, much less to investigate suburban gardens, since I'd gone there to watch a Saturday cricket match, but come Sunday morning I was up early and wandering around, and I came to an area tucked in between the M6 and the A57.

The area was being developed, or perhaps redeveloped. Whole new streets were being built – most of them looking very suburban – single-family, red-brick houses, some low-rise flats tucked in among the older high- or medium-rise blocks. Some streets were being renamed – there were signs up to that effect. One of the new names was Statham Street, named after the Lancashire cricketer Brian Statham. He retired in 1968 so there'd obviously been no great rush to memorialise him in these parts, though there *is* a Brian Statham Way that leads to the Old Trafford Cricket Ground. My immediate thought was that changing the names of streets must be a great annoyance for the inhabitants, postmen, visitors, and just about everyone.

The area was calm, quiet, unremarkable, until I came across an extraordinary garden belonging to an end-of-terrace house, older than the newbuilds, but not as old as all that. The garden was in two halves, one grass, one gravel, separated by a path. It was the most cluttered garden I've ever seen (Sir Francis Bacon would have had a fit at its busyness), with a dense clustering of pots containing hollyhocks, spurge, all kind of small flowering bedding plants, and then a vast sea of garden ornaments: an owl, a giraffe, a heron, a goose, a giant hedgehog, a minstrel, then a blue-painted bird bath, a blue-painted bench, a blue-painted swing seat. In fact there was so much going on that it had spilled out beyond the garden on to the shared green public patch outside, where there were more pots, a topiary arch and another bench, unpainted.

There was a man moving some of the pots around in the garden, and assuming he lived in the house, I asked him if it was OK for me to take a picture or two. He said it was fine by him, but it turned out he didn't live there, he was just a man come to mow the grass, and he had to move all the clutter off the lawn before he could start.

The actual inhabitant of the house came trotting out to see what was going on. She was a wiry, white-haired, old woman, Scottish as became obvious when she started to speak, and in her eighties as she told me immediately. I told her how much I liked her garden but she didn't want to talk about that, preferring to address broader subjects.

The ingratitude of youth was one of these. She'd had five children, all of them planned, and now had umpteen grandchildren and even more great grandchildren, and they all seemed to be spoiled and to have everything they wanted, and if you tried to give them a present all they wanted was money. And she did worry about what was happening to young people in general. She'd been back to Scotland and heard that lots of young people up there had committed suicide, and a lot of young people didn't care about anything. Like they were changing the street names in the area and the young people didn't seem bothered at all by it, but she was old and she was *really* bothered.

Drugs were another concern. There was a park opposite her house and at night, she said, it became a marketplace for the buying and selling of drugs.

'Everybody knows what's going on, including the police. But you never see a policeman. Not that I want to see a policemen …'

It was true enough that I hadn't seen a policeman on my meanderings that morning, but equally I hadn't seen any obvious druggies, and the area didn't appear to be ravaged by the drugs trade. I didn't doubt that young uns in the area were taking drugs, because that's what young uns do everywhere, but these did not feel or look like mean streets. The lady's garden seemed to confirm this. Surely such a well-loved and well-tended plot was the kind of thing that wicked druggies would have vandalised and destroyed. At the very least they'd have strewn it with syringes and nitrous vials. There was no evidence of this.

I didn't say that to the old lady. I didn't say much at all. She was doing all the talking. And then she said she didn't like people who were too quiet because you never knew what they were thinking. She may have had a point, but my quietness was partly because I couldn't get a word in, and largely because I didn't get the feeling she had the slightest interest in what I was thinking or what I might have to say. And this surely contradicts one of the received ideas about suburbia. OK, so people in suburbia may not want to know your innermost thoughts and philosophies, but they do want to know your *business*. The old lady never asked me what I was doing there, staring at her garden and taking photographs. She didn't ask where I was from, though she could obviously tell I wasn't a local. And if she had asked me what I was up to I'd have said something non-committal, that I was in town for the cricket match and was taking a Sunday morning walk to get a bit of fresh air. I definitely wouldn't have said I was investigating suburbia and writing a book about it. I would have lied. This meant that I was indeed closed up and hiding something, whereas she was open and hiding nothing. It seemed to me, that gave her quite a bit of moral advantage.

She started up again. 'Now I've got nothing against foreigners,' she said, a phrase that rarely precedes any noble utterance, 'but in those places over there,' and she gestured vaguely towards a block of flats on the other side of the park, 'they're all Pakistanis, and they all hate dogs, and I've got two of them.'

This had become apparent. A couple of big hounds with long black and white coats, maybe a sheepdog of some kind, were chasing around the garden and occasionally barking in my direction.

'I take my dogs for a walk in the park,' she continued, 'and they're always climbing up the trees trying to get away.'

It took me a little while to realise she meant it was the Pakistanis who were climbing the trees to get away from the dogs, rather than vice versa. I understand that the Koran has something to say about the unclean nature of dog saliva, and that much ritual cleansing is required if a dog dribbles on you.

'Anyway,' the old lady continued, 'I said to them, you lot eat dogs in your country, don't you?'

I would have thought the obvious contradictions of hating dogs and eating them would have been apparent even to someone without much interest in or knowledge of Islam, but maybe she was just joking about the whole thing. I do hope so.

God knows, I'm not the greatest lover of dogs, but in my wanderings around suburbia, if I climbed up a tree every time

I saw one, I might have turned into an Ewok by now. And if the Prophet's teaching is true that, 'Angels do not enter a house wherein there is a dog,' then suburbia must rarely be visited by angels. And, since the same bit of scripture has it that angels also decline to enter a house containing 'an animate picture' (and I'm assuming that means television) then I think we can safely assume that the suburbs are largely angel-free. Some of us are prepared to live with that state of affairs, though once in a while you do see a stone angel in amongst the gnomes.

8

The Garden Suburb

If you have an interest in the suburban garden you could do worse than visit a garden suburb. What I like best about Hampstead Garden Suburb is the name. It knows what it is, and it states the fact clearly and unashamedly. While so many places deny or try to disguise their suburban status, preferring to call themselves urban villages or luxury estates, Hampstead Garden Suburb doesn't pretend to be anything it isn't, and it embraces what it is. Having said that, it really doesn't resemble any other suburb I've ever been to. This, I would say, is an interesting contradiction.

If you go to Hampstead Garden Suburb by public transport, chances are you'll take the Tube, getting off at Golders Green station, and if there had been no Tube line, there might well never have been a Suburb. And there certainly wouldn't have been a suburb like this one if it hadn't been for Henrietta Barnett (1851–1936). Hampstead Garden Suburb was her creation, brainchild, pet project, her version of Arcadia.

She and her husband, the Reverend (later Canon) Samuel Barnett, owned a weekend house in Hampstead at Spaniards End (the apostrophe seems to come and go), and when they were on a trip to Russia in 1896 they met an American who predicted that before long there'd be a Tube station at the western edge of Hampstead Heath, close to where they lived. Henrietta didn't like that prospect, writing after the event,

> If this were to be so, it would result in the ruin of the sylvan restfulness of that portion of the most beautiful open space near London. The trains would also bring the builder, and it required no imagination to see the rows of ugly villas such as disfigure Willesden and most of the suburbs of London, in the foreground of that far-fetching and far-famed view.

She wasn't having any of that.

By any standards, Henrietta Barnett was a remarkable woman, if not by all accounts a particularly likeable one. She was a social reformer, author, a do-gooder – mostly in the best sense of the word – though she was known in some quarters as 'The Vicaress'. In August 1887 the Barnetts stayed with the economist and social reformer Beatrice Webb, who wrote in her diary:

> Mrs Barnett is an active-minded, true and warm-hearted woman. She is conceited. She would be objectionably conceited if it were not for her genuine belief in her husband's superiority…. The common opinion that a woman is a nonentity unless joined to a man, she resents

as a blasphemy. Like all crusaders, she is bigoted and does not recognise all the facts that tell against her faith. I told her that the only way in which we can convince the world of our power is to show it! And for that it will be needful for women with strong natures to remain celibate.

So, some contradictions there.

Details of Henrietta Barnett's early life are sketchy, but we know she was born in London, in Clapham, as Henrietta Rowland, daughter of a wealthy businessman, part of a family who'd made their fortune from the Macassar Oil Company. She spent much of her girlhood at her father's house in rural Kent, enjoying 'country pursuits', and had no formal education until she was sixteen when she spent just three terms at a school in Devon. It's hard to imagine that this background would have prepared her for many roles in life, but perhaps being a vicar's wife was one of them. When she was twenty she married Samuel Augustus Barnett, then curate of St Mary's, Bryanston Square, Marylebone, and no doubt the two of them could have led a very comfortable, ecclesiastical existence there, but they had a sense of duty, they wanted to do good, and they didn't mind making life hard for themselves. They asked for permission to reopen an abandoned church, St Jude's in Commercial Road, Whitechapel – St Jude is the patron saint of hope and impossible causes – and permission was duly granted.

Victorian philanthropy gets a mixed reception, often on the reasonable grounds that it was a form of condescension and social control, and I don't think the Barnetts were free from this. They were certain they knew what was best for the underclass. Still, if you wanted to make a difference why wouldn't you go to the place where a change in circumstances was most needed? Whitechapel was the worst of the worst at that time, the scene of terrible poverty, crime, violence, prostitution, appalling housing conditions, the streets running with slurry from slaughter houses, and soon to be the haunt of Jack the Ripper. One of the wilder conspiracy theories identifies Samuel Barnett as the Ripper. It's an unconvincing idea to my way of thinking, even if some of his writings about the vice to be seen on the streets of Whitechapel, including a description of women fighting in the street, topless, do strike a modern reader as distinctly prurient.

The cornerstone of the Barnetts' philosophy was what we might now call environmental determinism – a belief that an improvement in living conditions must inevitably lead to an improvement in morality, or at least in behaviour. They were very familiar with the forms of exploitation that went on in rented properties in their parish, and the debilitating and sometimes devastating effects it had on their parishioners.

The Barnetts worked hard in Whitechapel, and who can blame them if they sometimes retreated to their second home in Spaniards End? It was a long way from Whitechapel culturally if not geographically, although when they went there they often took guests with them, some deserving cases from Whitechapel. Henrietta wrote, 'a few days or weeks at Hampstead became a joy to many weary people of all classes'.

Having noted the warning about the Tube, and realising that its arrival was inevitable, she decided that rather than let some speculative builder buy up the land at the western end of Hampstead Heath and plant houses on it, she'd acquire the land herself and build her own suburban utopia there. It's hard to see this as an entirely altruistic act: she obviously didn't want to live next to an ugly suburban housing estate, but then how many do?

Henrietta Barnett was in some sense a socialist. She wrote a number of books with her husband, including *Practicable Socialism* (1889) and *Towards Social Reform* (1909). It was not hard to imagine better social arrangements than existed in Whitechapel at that time, but she had no experience of building a suburb from scratch. How many people do? She was fifty-two years old at this point, and her husband, supportive as he was, thought this was too big a task for her to take on at that stage of her life. Little did he know.

The first part of the plan was to set up a trust to acquire the land, 243 acres which belonged to Eton College. Although Henrietta had a reputation for being autocratic, it became clear that she wasn't going to be able to bulldoze the men from Eton. The Eton trustees explicitly said they didn't think a woman would be able to manage such a large estate, but they didn't dismiss her entirely. They said they were prepared to reconsider, giving her an option to purchase if she had some men of substance backing her up. This was sexist and patronizing, of course, but in the circumstances it turned out to be useful advice.

By her own account she put together a 'veritable showman's happy family' of the great and the good, lawyers, men of the Church, a few men with titles: Lord Crew, Earl Grey, Sir John Gorst, Sir Robert Spencer, the Bishop of London. However these were merely figureheads who would have little real involvement with, or control over, the project. Their presence satisfied Eton, the sale went through. The Suburb would be all hers.

She enlisted architects Unwin and Parker of Letchworth Garden City fame to plan and design her suburb. This time, unlike at Letchworth, Unwin was the prime mover, and he wrote in 1911 in *Garden Cities & Town Planning Magazine*:

It was regarded by Mrs Barnett as one of the most important parts of the scheme, from the social point of view, that
all classes should be housed within the area of the estate.
Thoughtful people who have had experience of large towns
in the neighbourhood, of which there have been growing
up vast suburbs often peopled by one class or another of
the community, have realised the very grave evils resulting
from this aggregation of people having such a one-sided
and limited outlook on life. And while it is obviously not
possible to mix together indiscriminately the dwellings

of people of all classes, the promoters of the suburb felt that a great effort should be made to prove that it is not only possible, but that it is in every way most desirable.

As this suggests, socialist or not, Henrietta Barnett never intended that Hampstead Garden Suburb would be a haven of classless egalitarianism. Rather it would be a place where different classes learned to get along. Right from the beginning, designs showed houses of different sizes, quality and prices, which could be sold or rented to people in accordance with their differing needs and incomes.

Henrietta Barnett also employed the architects M.H. Baillie Scott, Charles Cowles-Voysey and Geoffrey Lucas to design different building types, and she roped in Edwin Lutyens, initially as a consultant, but before long he was a fully hands-on architect for the project.

Lutyens had, at best, mixed feelings about Henrietta Barnett, and wrote in a letter to his wife, 'nice woman … but proud of being a philistine who had no idea beyond a window box full of geraniums, calceolarias and lobelias, over which you can see a goose on the green'. Lutyens knew about gardens, having worked extensively with the garden designer Gertrude Jekyll. He also wanted there to be shops in the suburb, but Henrietta Barnett was having none of that, nor was she having cafés or pubs, a cinema, or anything else that sounded like too much fun. She is on record as saying she wanted to build a theatre, but it would have proved too expensive. This lack of facilities would obviously have consequences for the Suburb: it was never going to be self-sufficient or self-contained. Even if the residents were tee-totallers, never ate out, and never went to see films, they'd still have to leave the suburb to buy groceries, for instance, and of course they also had to leave in order to go to work.

The Trust formally purchased the land in 1906, and, on 2 May 1907, Henrietta Barnett broke ground on the site. There were speeches, some poetry was read, and there was dancing around a maypole. Two cottages were built on the site where that opening ceremony took place: 140 and 142 Hampstead Way, completed in October 1908. Large numbers of houses, maisonettes and flats were soon built, in all about 5,000 properties housing around 13,000 people. More land was purchased, to the east of the original site, eventually extending to 800 acres. For all Henrietta's guidance, this development was largely taken care of by the private sector. Some houses were built to order for owner-occupiers, while other developers saw that they could make money by building to rent. There was also some shared housing for single men and women: 'Residences' for the middle class, 'Hostels' for the lower orders.

Henrietta Barnett established an outdoor gym and encouraged gardening – starting the HGS Horticultural Society (which sounds much grander than a gardening club). She was in favour of certain kinds of sport, so opportunities existed for tennis, cricket, bowls, croquet, cycling, even billiards, but she wasn't so keen on football, neither rugby nor soccer, so there were no facilities for those. She set up the Suburb Institute – a college much like any other in many respects, with classes in first aid, foreign languages, remedial reading and maths, though these last two didn't get many takers. We might guess that if people were smart enough to get themselves into the Suburb they knew how to read, write and add up.

In an article titled 'Science and City Suburbs', published in *Public Affairs* magazine in 1906 Henrietta Barnett wrote:

Cities must grow. The progress of mankind is from the Garden of Eden to the City of God. Cities must grow, but it is the gift of science that the growth may be so directed that the citizen may have both the inspiration of a garden and the stimulus of a living community.

As I set off to visit, this struck me as a lot to ask of any city.

My friend Joanna Moriarty grew up in Hampstead Garden Suburb, and she has two stories that epitomize the place for her. The first involves somebody from the Hampstead Garden Suburb Trust hammering on the front door of the family house one weekend afternoon, and saying to her father, 'Your next door neighbour is laying crazy paving! What are you going to do about it?'

Crazy paving, evidently was (and very probably still is) anathema to the aesthetes of Hampstead Garden Suburb. However, Joanna's dad, being an English gent of the old school, said simply, 'I'm going to continue to mind my own business,' which is what most suburbanites want, or at least claim to want.

The second story involves a joke, which I think is told about places other than the Suburb but it still works. It concerns a man who's shipwrecked on a desert island, a place that somehow has lots of building materials, and a place so large that over the years, while he's marooned, he's able to build himself a whole town, perhaps complete with suburbs.

When a rescue party finally arrives, the rescuers are amazed by what he's created, and they ask him to give them a tour of this island town, which he's happy to do. As they walk around, he indicates the various buildings he's made, and at one point he says, 'That's the church I go to,' and then he turns and points in the other direction, and says, 'And that's the church I *don't* go to.'

I'm not saying it's a hilarious joke, but it applies with strange precision to the situation in Hampstead Garden Suburb. At the heart of things is Central Square, a broad, green patch of land, a sort of public garden, and on opposite sides, facing each other, are St Jude's Church and the Hampstead Garden Suburb Free Church, both of them designed by Lutyens. The Henrietta Barnett School takes up another side of the square. The Free Church has an inscription in stone that reads, 'God is greater than the creeds,' a theological proposition I don't feel qualified to explicate, but I do know that the *Manchester Guardian* described the church as an 'experiment' and 'the most original church in or near London. The foundation is not less original for the fact that there is no other interdenominational Free Church in the country.' To be fair, there is now also a Quaker Meeting House and a synagogue in Hampstead Garden Suburb, though they weren't established until the 1930s, and they certainly weren't designed by an architect of Lutyens's status.

Since the gardens are obviously so important, so much a part of the Suburb's self-definition, I decided to go there on a Sunday when the Suburb was taking part in the National Open Garden Scheme. You make outsiders pay for the privilege of being allowed into your garden. It's for charity.

I always enjoy being nosy, peering over fences, looking into people's gardens, but this time it was sanctioned and encouraged. You were allowed to be *really* nosy, to go up and down the garden paths, examine the plantings, poke around, take pictures, see the owners in their natural habitat, and talk to them.

Walking from Golders Green Tube and entering the Suburb, anyone's first impression is likely to be that there are a vast number of places in the world that seem much more thoroughly suburban than this one. True, most of the houses have their own substantial plots, there's plenty of greenery, you couldn't pretend it's the inner city, you definitely could pretend it's the country, and yet it doesn't feel like the average, or even the better than average, suburb.

Partly, perhaps mostly, it's because of the type and quality of the buildings. The houses tend to be older, solid, traditional, a lot of red brick, a lot of swooping tile roofs, some elaborate chimney stacks. Some of these are no doubt by Lutyens, though I couldn't swear which ones were real Lutyens and which were in the *style* of Lutyens. Incidentally, Joanna told me that the word on the street was that if you bought a Lutyens house you were

buying yourself a world of trouble. Those roofs were considered
to be a serious liability.

There are plenty of detached houses, some terraces, and only a
minority of the houses are semi-detached, although, as we know,
the first houses ever built in the Suburb *are* semis: 140 and 142
Hampstead Way. They're still there, looking much as they always
did, at least from the outside, substantial, angular, not red brick
but white painted rendering. They look like mirror images of
each other. When I was there, 140 had a memorial plaque, 142
had a burglar alarm, they had different chimney-pots but otherwise I couldn't see any differences. Nobody had been making
improvements or 'expressing' themselves by adding extensions,
porches or new kinds of window. This is probably because the
Trust wouldn't allow them to.

The overall feel of the Suburb, and I know this is a minefield,
is that everything looks more elegant, more 'tasteful' (also of
course more expensive) than the average suburban enclave. The
cars were fancy, plenty of Mercedes and Porsches, quite a few
with personalised number plates, and one house had a Jaguar
hearse parked out front, which is a thing you don't see every day.

The front gardens were worked on, and individualistic to an
extent, although again nobody had expressed wild eccentricity.
There were shrubs, herbaceous borders, quite a few gardens had
plants trained into geometrical shapes, some forming archways
over the garden gate. One or two front gardens had been paved
over to provide parking for the fancy cars, but fewer than in
many suburbs I've been to. There were lots of hedges – and it
took me longer than it probably should have to realise there are
no garden walls in Hampstead Garden Suburb, again the Trust
doesn't permit such things.

Naturally, on the day I went, the gardens were looking their
best. I'm sure a vast amount of work goes into making things
look just right for this single day. And the owners were on their
best behaviour too, standing in their gardens, very welcoming,

very easy to talk to, some very posh indeed, some not posh at all. I suppose you have to be friendly and outgoing if you're inviting the public into your garden, but most were warmer and chattier than they needed to be. They seemed knowledgeable without being know-it-alls. Maybe there was a bit of showing off, demonstrating that they had better gardens than their neighbours, but it didn't seem especially pernicious. They were happy to talk about their gardens, happy to recount stories from previous years, such as the one about a member of the public who was found asleep in various corners of several different gardens in the course of the afternoon.

As is usually the case, there was more eccentricity in the back gardens than in the front: one had a memorial to a family's pet dogs, one had an apple tree that looked as ancient as Eden, there were a surprising number of ponds. There were pieces of statuary and hardware: stone lions, greyhounds, chimney pots, one garden that described itself as having *objets trouvés* which included bollards. If there were gnomes, I didn't see them.

I did feel that, in the leaflet and map that helped you find your way around and described the gardens, some of the owners were overselling the attractions of their plots. One claimed to have 'a sinuous lawn', another claimed to have a woodland garden, which turned out to consist of dead tree branches interspersed with foxgloves, and quite a few boasted that they'd been given Suburb in Bloom awards.

There were a lot of little alleyways running between the houses and gardens. These were lined with hedges of course, not walls, and I had it explained to me that in these parts they were known as twittens. This isn't a pure Hampstead Garden Suburb word, it seems to be Sussex dialect and how it came to be a Suburb word I'm not sure.

Everything in the Garden Suburb was lovely, if neither quite the Garden of Eden nor the City of God. It seemed like it would be a good enough place to live, not that there was the slightest chance of my living there. I had moved to my own suburban house in Essex because it had been an affordable option. That didn't apply to Hampstead Garden Suburb. There was an enormous premium for living here. It was part of London, and the centre was easily accessible, but it didn't *feel* much like London, which I think is exactly what Henrietta Barnett would have wanted.

9

Sitcom Suburbia

Not everything that happens in the suburbs is a suitable subject for comedy. Not every piece of comedy is suitable for inclusion in a sitcom. Not all sitcoms are set in suburbia. But when the circles on the Venn diagram overlap, we arrive at the suburban sitcom, a specialised, powerful and surprisingly varied form. At the moment it may not be deeply fashionable but nevertheless it's a form that endures and that's provided the world with a pretty good number of pretty good television shows about the pleasures and problems of quotidian domestic life.

It's hard to imagine any comedy that doesn't in some way involve a 'situation' but the term sitcom as we understand it only came into general use in the 1950s. *Pinwright's Progress* has some claim to have been the first TV sitcom, with ten shows broadcast by the BBC in 1946 and '47, but it was set in a shop rather than a suburb, and, in any case, no episodes are known to survive. *I Love Lucy* began in the US in 1951, and continued until 1957, which I believe makes it the first true American sitcom, and it did feature a mixed-race couple which put it ahead of the game in all kinds of ways, however it was mostly set in a New York City apartment. Only towards the end of the run did the Ricardos move to Westport in Connecticut, and they stayed there for the next version of the show *The Lucille Ball–Desi Arnaz Comedy Hour* (1957–60). Today Westport is a much richer suburb than it was then, but at the time it even had some rural elements: one episode of the show involves Lucy raising chickens. This was never a show that strove for strict social realism but the move to Westport did echo a trend in the real American world: a lot of people were leaving New York City for the suburbs. The show's producers could see plenty of mileage in Lucy as a fish out of water in suburbia, though the show was much less popular than when it had been set in New York.

For comedy writers, then and still to some extent now, the suburbs are a natural and perhaps neutral territory. There's a sense that the things happening there are not quite serious, and although people have problems (no problems means there's no show), they're ones that can, in some fashion or other, be resolved by the end of the half-hour episode. This may suggest that life in suburbia is fundamentally easy, or downright unserious, but at least it's funny, at least some of the time.

If you were looking for an avatar of British suburban comedy, then it seems to me that Terry Scott would do nicely. After a substantial career appearing on stage, in films that included Carry Ons, in a few sitcoms with Hugh Lloyd (*Hugh and I*, and *Hugh and I Spy* among them), and in sketch shows, Scott found himself opposite June Whitfield first in *Happy Ever After*, that ran from 1974 to 1979, and then in a rejigged version as *Terry and June*, that ran from 1979 to 1987. The shows became the archetypal, stereotypical British suburban sitcom, which is not necessarily a compliment. The fact that millions of people watched, apparently with pleasure, might even have been part of the problem: the concept was too mainstream, too conventional, too obvious, too square; just like the suburbs themselves.

I know that Terry Scott still has his fans, but for my money he comes across as unfunny and, perhaps just as important, unlikeable. He's the 'typical' husband and father (the daughter is absent from the show), the breadwinner, the king of the castle who is nevertheless a stranger in his own home, frustrated and powerless. He's a man-child, dissatisfied with the way the world works, though peevish and fussy rather than genuinely angry, someone who has to be indulged and placated. This might be to say that he's simply a prime representative of patriarchy, and this hardly makes him a unique figure in the world of sitcoms. In turn, his wife June, played by June Whitfield, who is conspicuously cleverer, wiser, more level-headed than her husband, is the one who has to do the indulging and placating. This could be seen as very dodgy even in those unenlightened times.

There's an extraordinary episode of *Terry and June* titled 'Writing on the Wall' (1979). The McGuffin is the sudden appearance of obscene graffiti on the garden wall belonging to the neighbours who live across the street from Terry and June. We're never allowed to see the graffiti, not even told what the words are, except that in Terry's opinion it's 'filth, verbal filth', and that it's also misspelled. The perpetrator is referred to at one point as 'the filthy phantom.'

The neighbours are Tina and Brian Pillbeam, less middle class than Terry and June. Tina wears high heels and leopard-skin prints, so you know she's no better than she ought to be. The Pillbeams aren't too upset by the graffiti, because it's on the front of their garden wall, so that when they look out of their windows they can't see it. The problem seems to be all Terry's, and to a much lesser extent June's. She's far more phlegmatic about these things, although Terry demonstrates a need to protect her, the delicate, sensitive woman, from seeing bad language.

Quite coincidentally, the Pillbeams have Tina's twelve-year-old nephew Magnus staying with them. The lad is small, shy, bespectacled, and barely capable of speaking to adults. Will it surprise you that he turns out to be the filthy phantom?

The episode is overloaded with other plot elements, but the graffiti are at the centre, and in this context they're an especially potent and troubling problem because they're an indication that what might be thought of as inner-city problems can sometimes be found in suburbia. What's the point of being in the suburbs if you have urban problems? The fact that young Magnus is as suburban as can be, and in no way resembles an inner-city youth, might be used to give the issue some extra spin, as might his problems with spoken as opposed to written communication, but the writer of the episode, John Kean, lets those details go by. In the end, for reasons too wearying to go into, Terry gets towed away in a one-man model of the Starship Enterprise. Really. I found the whole thing excruciating, though millions of viewers would no doubt once have disagreed with me.

The longevity of the *Terry and June* format seems even more surprising when you remember that other, much fresher, models were available at the time. *The Good Life* (1975–78) poked topical fun at ideas of self-sufficiency by imagining it in suburbia, specifically Surbiton. In other contexts its star Richard Briers had been the ultimate, tame suburban husband, but here he's Tom, the eccentric man in a mid-life crisis who's decided to become a sort of hippy. He's quit his job, paid off his mortgage and is planning, with his wife Barbara, to live off the land, growing vegetables and raising livestock, bartering whenever he can.

Surbiton does occupy this strange place in comedy circles: I think it's the name that does it. It's already halfway to sounding like 'suburb' and that reinforces its reputation as the ultimate, most mockable and laughable suburb.* Yet in some ways this is unfair. Norbiton, which is no distance away, doesn't experience that same intense, dismissive suburban identification, even though Surb and Norb, are just prefixes meaning south and north, and frankly there are some comedy writers who'd consider 'Norb' comedy gold. Norbition is in fact the station where Reginald Perrin gets on his commuter train in *The Fall and Rise of Reginald Perrin* (1976–79), a comedy based on the novel by David Nobbs, about a man faking his own death rather than facing up to his suburban responsibilities.

Yet another model is *George and Mildred* (1976–79), a spin off from *Man About the House* (which was set in London), and it featured the couple of the title moving to a modern, expensive housing estate in Hampton Wick, yep that's an example of the humour, where they're regarded as vulgarians, in danger of bringing down the tone of the neighbourhood.

Before that, *Love Thy Neighbour* (1972–76 – there was a feature film in 1973) had tackled, albeit ham-fistedly, the racism encountered by a Black family that moves into a white suburb, a show which even at the time was criticised for its dubious racial politics.

Still at least you might say that all these shows suggested in their different, more or less successful, more or less subtle, ways that life in suburbia isn't always entirely calm, quiet, untroubled and apolitical but these sitcoms came and went, as for that matter did the 'alternative comedy' of *The Young Ones* (1982–84) even as *Terry and June* rolled on.

*

---

* I do keep wondering how significant it is that two of the authors I liked best as a child, Alfred Bestall, writer and illustrator (though not creator) of Rupert Bear, and Enid Blyton, creator of Noddy, the Secret Seven, the Famous Five and many, many more, both lived in Surbition at one time or another. Did their suburban values trickle down into their work, and then tinge my childhood with suburban dreams and aspirations?

Showbiz magic constantly transmutes the geography of suburbia. Terry and June lived at 71 Poplar Avenue, Purley, Surrey
(a fictional address). The location for the outdoor shots was
actually The Avenue, Sutton, Surrey. The titles show Terry using
the station at East Croydon, a few miles away from both Purley
and Sutton, the kind of distance a commuter might tolerate.

The Good Life was set in Surbiton, though it was filmed in
Northwood. Reginald Perrin's house was in Coleridge Road, part
of the fictional Poets' Estate, in the equally fictional Climthorpe,
but the show was filmed in the perfectly real Ealing. In *Love Thy
Neighbour* the Booths and the Reynoldses live in a supposedly
working-class part of Twickenham; the exterior shots were filmed
in Teddington.

All of which seems to suggest that sitcom suburbia is a kind
of homogenised no man's land, where one place is just as good
as another. It will also be obvious that these suburbias are all in
the south of England and either close to or in London. *Keeping
up Appearances* (1990–95), again a comedy about suburban class
and snobbery, was filmed in and around the West Midlands, but
that's about as far north as the suburban sitcom goes, even if non
suburban sitcoms such as *The Likely Lads* (1964–66, 1973–74)
were set further afield.

Two of the most genuinely subversive British comedies set
in suburbia – *Stella Street* (1997–2001) and *Suburban Shootout*
(2006–7) – don't stray too far from the southeast. The women
in *Suburban Shootout* are the antithesis of Stepford wives: members of rival female gangs which operate in the fictional suburb
of Little Steppington; most of the filming was done in Pinner.

The premise of *Stella Street* was that the likes of Mick Jagger
and David Bowie (and anybody else who could be convincingly
impersonated by Phil Cornwell and John Sessions) were tired of
the glamorous, showbiz life, and, in search of a more ordinary,
more authentic suburban existence, had moved to a place called
Suburbiton, a not even remotely veiled reference to Surbiton.

*

In the United States they do things differently in some ways, but not so very differently in others. There are, however, two major and conspicuous differences between British and American suburban sitcoms.

The first is longevity: *Everybody Loves Raymond* (1996–2005), set on suburban Long Island, ran for 210 episodes; *King of Queens* (1998–2007), set in the New York borough of the title, ran for 206. *Modern Family* (2009–20) a skillfully made show set in an all-purpose, prosperous Los Angeles, with exteriors shot in Cheviot Hills, was a bit of a sheep in wolf's clothing. It featured a gay married couple with an adopted Vietnamese daughter (though the actress who latterly played her was Korean-American), a family patriarch who was married to a Columbian spitfire, but the show nevertheless felt resolutely middle of the road: it reached 250 episodes. Despite how long *Terry and June* lasted, there are only 65 episodes, and only 30 of *The Good Life*.

The second is the more persistent presence and exploration of racial anxieties. In recent years a number of American suburban sitcoms have centred around non-white characters and their problems, and these problems include, though are not limited to, the effects of suburbia on people of colour, these effects being very different from those experienced by white people. *The Cosby Show* opened the way, though the Cosbies lived in Greenwich Village, about as urban as it gets. However, the show also featured, as have a high proportion of subsequent shows of this kind, a Black family that has moved into the upper middle class.

Bill Cosby (if we can mention him) was Cliff Huxtable, a doctor, and it was his profession that allowed him to move up the social ladder. Will Smith, in *The Fresh Prince of Bel Air* (1990–96), took a different route, where the transition was as easy as it was unlikely. His presence in the wealthy suburb of the title was a kind of residential rehab. Having got into teenage trouble in his home city of Philadelphia, he'd been sent to live with his wealthy uncle, a lawyer, whose job it was to straighten him out. The clash between assimilated and unassimilated Black characters, between street and suburbia, gave the show much of its impetus, although nobody ever accused it of being completely credible.

Different improbabilities inhabit *Black-ish* (2014 onwards). The central character here, the father of the family, is Andre 'Dre' Johnson, played by Anthony Anderson, an advertising executive, successful enough to own a grand colonial-style suburban house in Sherman Oaks, Los Angeles. But Dre is from Compton and he worries that his kids are losing their cultural heritage, their Blackness, by living in the white suburbs. The show has won a roomful of awards, even as certain critics have objected to the idea that Black culture will be diminished by exposure to whiteness. I've been trying to imagine a sitcom based on the opposite racial premise, and have realised that no good will come of that.

The characters in *Fresh Off the Boat* (2015 onwards) – based on the memoir of chef and food writer Eddie Huang, who is also a qualified lawyer – have different worries, but since the parents come originally from Taiwan, and have recently moved to Orlando, Florida, from Washington DC, the issue of assimilation is of a different kind. Fitting in is at least as important as retaining their culture, because fitting in is how they plan to rise in America.

Here the father is not in the same social bracket as doctor, lawyer or advertising executive, but rather the owner of a cowboy-themed steakhouse. The show is filmed a long way from Florida. The exterior of the family home is in Mar Vista, in LA: the location used for the steakhouse is a Thai restaurant in Glendale, strictly speaking just outside LA. The double fakery might briefly tempt you to think this was some Baudrillard-style simulacrum, but only briefly.

*

A recent English sitcom, *Home* (2019 onwards), on the surface seems to offer a fresh take on race and class in the English suburbs. Sami Ibrahim, a refugee from Syria, in his mid-thirties, has made his way into England by hiding in the boot of the car belonging to Katie and Peter, a couple who live in a pleasant detached house in Dorking. He's a quantity surveyor, she's a teacher.

Rather than hand Sami over to the authorities they let him live with them while his application for political asylum is being processed. Sami is also a teacher, well-educated, Shakespeare-quoting, and able to tutor Katie and Peter's son. Meanwhile we discover that Sami's own son and wife are in Berlin, living with a heart-surgeon and his wife. Complications ensue, Sami gets the hots for Katie, and there's a big question of whether the family will reunite, and if so will it be in Dorking or Berlin.

These are not the issues faced by Terry and June, nor by Lucy and Desi for that matter, so you have to give the show some credit for expanding the sitcom universe; on the other hand, it doesn't really seem that Sami's problems, experienced while living in haute suburbia, are quite the ones most Syrian refugees have to deal with.

All this reliance on economic success and upward mobility might make you nostalgic for a simpler, less materialistic, less late-capitalist time, the era when a sitcom might be set in a rag and bone yard, as in *Steptoe and Son* (1962–65 and 1970–74), or in a junk yard as in *Sanford and Son* (1972–77), the American version based on it. The Sanford junkyard was in LA, in Watts, at 9114 South Central Avenue: a real place. It's an area that resists gentrification but still looks quite suburban to British eyes. The *Steptoe and Son* yard was in Shepherd's Bush in the fictional Oil Drum Lane.

There was a big difference of emphasis in the characters of the English and American versions, first of course Sanford and his Son were Black. Beyond that, Redd Foxx played the cankerous, scheming father who regularly got into trouble, and was helped out of it by his son, but the son had already moved up in the world. In *Steptoe and Son,* although Harold had aspirations and the urge to better himself, these plans were constantly being thwarted by his dad, Albert. There is one episode, however, where suburbia figures front and centre.

The episode title is 'Without Prejudice' (1970). It is, naturally enough, about prejudice, though of the class rather than the racial kind. Harold wants to move into suburbia, so he and his dad go to look at a suburban semi-detached house that's up for sale. This being a comedy show, they go there by horse and cart, horrifying the neighbours who eventually pay them not to move in. The last scene has Albert thinking this might be a great money-making scheme. I suppose that if the Steptoes had been Black this plotline would have been too contentious, even in 1970.

There are times when the suburban sitcom feels like an historical form, and one that is perhaps coming to its natural end. It's not hard to think of reasons for this. The first might be that suburban worries now seem trivial and have been superseded by much greater and less comical ones. It's hard to get terribly upset about your neighbour failing to return the lawnmower when the news on climate change is that before long the lawn will either be under water or turned into a piece of scorched earth. This is not an issue that will be solved by the end of the episode of any sitcom. Equally shows like *The Office, Parks and Recreation* and *Fleabag,* don't deal with suburban life at all, even if some of the characters may well be suburbanites.

Perhaps the next great sitcom will be set in a Japanese ghost home, in a clothing-optional gated community or in a mega-suburb in Brazil. There have been worse premises. In any event, there's a case to be made that all the best suburban sitcoms aren't *really* about suburbia at all, and that ones that are *actually* about suburbia often purport to be about something else.

In *The Addams Family* TV show (1964–66) a bunch of ghouls move into a gothic house in an otherwise ordinary suburban neighbourhood. They're one more group of outsiders trying to assimilate themselves, and they're baffled by the consternation they cause to their neighbours. My ex-wife loved it when she was growing up. She said she always regarded her own weirdo, misfit family as the Addamses of *her* neighbourhood, and she took enormous comfort from the show.

In *The Simpsons*, the town of Springfield is infinitely malleable, a place where the writers can insert a desert or a fireworks factory or a monorail, as required. For all the mayhem, and a certain amount of world travel, the Simpsons remain rooted in their surprisingly large, detached house with its two-car garage, in the thoroughly suburban Evergreen Terrace, but it's not a show *about* suburbia. It's a show that can be about anything the writers choose to make it about.

And sometimes it's the other way round. Another animated cartoon that played magnificently with the notions of suburbia was *The Flintstones* (1960–66). The show found Stone Age equivalents for all the features of 1960s American suburbs: the foot-driven car, the house made of rocks, the pet dinosaur. Was this a depiction of suburbia? Well, it certainly wasn't a depiction of the Stone Age. The same point could be made about *The Jetsons* – suburbia in space.

My favourite line in *The Flintstones* comes from Wilma when she is complaining to husband Fred about how boring her existence is, 'I work hard all day too, and what do I get? A lot of yak from you. You at least get out every day, see things, talk to people. I never get out of this cave.'

That's very funny and it's *very* suburban.

10

Suburban Spreads

Is there such a thing as 'suburban food'? Obviously I'm inclined to think so, otherwise I wouldn't be writing a chapter about it, but I also think it's very hard to define and that it comes in various and sometimes contradictory forms.

In one sense everything eaten in the suburbs must by one definition be suburban food, but it isn't that straightforward. What people do and can eat in the suburbs is limited by availability, by what's on offer, as much as by their tastes, by their deepest needs and appetites. My own small suburb offers nowhere to buy food, unless you count the occasional visit by an ice-cream van, but outside the suburb the Co-op supermarket is only a ten-minute walk or three-minute drive away. You'll find it hard to buy a really good piece of fish there but you'll find any number of ready meals, and on the right day there'll be some decent meat and poultry, even game. The ready meals may seem more obviously suburban than the game, but that's to impose some prejudices on what we think suburbanites eat. Moreover, on Saturdays there's a farmers' market near by. People go there to buy oysters, samphire, wild rabbit, Italian salamis and cheeses. I'm one of these people. So, by the time I've got them back to my suburban house, have they become suburban foods? And if not then what would *make* them suburban foods? The addition of a Kraft cheese slice? A blob of ketchup? A side-order of potato wedges? These prejudices are hard to shake.

There's a tendency to believe that the food of the past is laughable and absurd, that it's the food of our unknowing and unsophisticated ancestors, and suburban food especially may often be considered synonymous with naffness and kitsch, so that a description of suburban food can become a menu of all the unfashionable foods we may have eaten, and even enjoyed, when we were younger and had less educated palates, foods that we like to think we've outgrown.

The internet is full of lurid photographs of food from the past, many of which might have seemed perfectly appetizing at the time. My own list of such foods might include luncheon meat fritters, Fray Bentos steak-and-kidney pudding in a tin, suet pudding, potted meat, fry up, haslet. My mother served these things up without embarrassment or apology, and with the sense that she was doing her best for her family. But these categories of naffness and kitsch are very unstable. The suburban menu is being constantly modified. Tiramisu was once an exotic treat you only had in an upmarket Italian restaurant; now you can find it in the chill cabinet of most supermarkets. Just occasionally it goes the other way. Devilled eggs, for instance, which strike me as utterly suburban, can now be found on the menus of some very hip restaurants. Eccles cakes which I grew up eating as a rather unexciting dessert, are regularly on the menu at Fergus Henderson's reataurant St John, served with a slice of Lancashire cheese.

As this suggests, there's considerable back and forth between public and private eating. People who live in the suburbs don't spend all their time eating there. They go out for meals, in most cases leaving their suburb, although there are certain suburbs large enough to contain a variety of 'suburban restaurants', a term that needs further definition. In any case, when suburbanites go out they don't usually want to eat the same things as when they're at home, if they did there'd be no point in going out.

I think, for example, that the people in my own suburb don't eat much sushi because there isn't a Japanese restaurant to hand, though there are several in Colchester, about ten miles away. Are people from suburbia the customers who frequent Colchester's Wagamama and Tokyo Sizzle? Well, I'm guessing a good proportion of them must be. So does that mean that gyozas and ramen are now suburban foods? Maybe. Certainly pot noodles, which once might have seemed wildly exotic under the name ramen, now seem thoroughly suburban and have been for a few decades.

Again, easy walking distance from where I live, but outside the suburb itself, there's a fish-and-chip shop, but it's hard to think of fish and chips as exactly suburban food: it's every bit as urban as it is suburban. There's also a nearby Bangladeshi restaurant, a fancy Italian place, a wine-cum-tapas bar, as well as several other takeaways, and most of these establishments will gladly deliver to your suburb if it's not too far away. So all this I suppose must also be a form of suburban food too.

These things are also culturally specific. I remember on my first trip to the United States, while I was a student, I went to an Arthur Treacher's Fish and Chip restaurant; the fish and chips weren't good at all, but I also ate 'chips and dip' – potato crisps with which you scooped up some inscrutable but very tasty, not so say, downright addictive, white glop. It seemed as sinful as it did exotic. At the time I had very little idea what I was eating, and I did wonder what kind of culture I had entered that thought crisps needed to be livened up with a semi-solid dip. In fact I was just showing my alien ignorance. I now know that I was eating 'California Dip', which Mike and Jane Stern, two very shrewd observers of American life and food culture, consider the archetypal suburban food. The 'recipe' involves taking a pint of sour cream and adding a packet of dried onion soup mix. That's it, simple. As a matter of fact I had it not that long ago at a party in California, by then it had become retro and ironic. And no less addictive.

But in truth, the early suburbanites who embraced California Dip were, it seems, part of a cultural avant-garde, also perhaps the victims of Big Food. Sour cream was a tough sell in America. Who wanted their cream to be sour? The Sterns write in *The Lexicon of Real American Food* (2011), 'California made it [sour cream] a staple of suburban cookery, paving the way for America's home epicures to embrace beef stroganoff, sour cream Jell-O molds, and sour cream cheesecake.' It was all a plot to sell more sour cream in the suburbs; and it worked.

While I was fretting about what suburban food might or might not be, I found online a 2012 MA thesis from the University of Colorado by Jessica Sharon Partridge (did I say something about names being destiny?) titled *Tasting Suburbia: American Cookbooks and the Environment, 1949–87*. It sounded promising, not least since collecting eccentric cookery books is one of my more innocent obsessions.

Since you ask, one of my prizes is *Good Housekeeping's Vegetarian Recipes*, 1956, price one shilling and sixpence. It contains recipes for dishes such as Stuffed French Loaf, Nut Dumpling, Celery Hotpot and, best of all, Japanese Salad: a slice of pineapple on a lettuce leaf, topped with pieces of tomato, orange and pear, and 'other fresh fruits as available,' garnished with whipped cream or watercress. How many of these delights were really eaten in suburbia I'm not sure. But I digress.

Sharon Partridge writes, 'American cookbooks are discursive texts that simultaneously support and challenge the suburban ideal,' which sounds great even if she then admits, 'The suburban ideal has no concrete definition.' Not that she needs one since 'this sample confirms the capacity of cookbooks as sites of historical, social, and environmental engagement and investigation, and reveals American foodways and the suburban environments they represent as manifestations of desires to separate human life and culture from the natural world.'

I was a little disappointed to find that the 'cohort' (her term) of books discussed consisted of just eleven volumes, but then again I was encouraged by the presence of Thomas Mario's *The Playboy Gourmet* (1961), a source of considerable entertainment and amusement under the Nicholson roof. It's not to be taken too seriously or at face value, but it's not quite the vacuous celebration of the *Playboy* philosophy you might expect: some of the recipes are perfectly good. It seems to me however, that it's thoroughly *antisuburban*, written for the real or (more likely) wannabe swinging urban bachelor, preparing steak and lobster for his hot date. You can probably imagine how this book would currently be received in American Academia, and like many academics Ms Partridge is a bit of a scold.

She's dismayed to find that the values and prejudices espoused in old cookbooks don't entirely coincide with her own, although I think most of us would share her dismay at cookbooks ostensibly designed to catch and keep a man; and yes, there does seem to be something rather suburban and offensive about this idea, though who knows if it worked. I wonder if anyone has done research comparing suburban marital breakdown with suburban wives' ability to follow recipes.

But what Partridge really hates, a little surprisingly in this context, is lawns. She writes, 'According to NASA, the amount of land devoted to grass lawns in 2005 in the US was three times the amount of land devoted to corn. This loss of agricultural land to suburban sprawl and its attendant lawns impacts American foodways by narrowing the available options for food and increasing the distance between people and the natural world.' I bow to nobody in my distrust of suburban lawns but I never realised that the problem was that they were narrowing my available food options. On the other hand my own front garden, which might once have been a lawn, is currently overgrown with brambles, so I do get my share of blackberries from the earth. I'm not sure if that counts as a foodway.

Partridge does at least show a sense of humour when the writers of her cookbooks do.

> Mary Meade [she writes] has a fondness for molds – not the biological variety, but the gelatin 'salad' kind – and the supermarket is something like an experimental treasure hunt for new combinations of ingredients for these creations. There is her famous lime gelatin with avocado, onions, and pickled beets; her blue cheese gelatin mold with pecans, served with fresh fruit, her allegedly refreshing Jellied olive and Grapefruit salad. Be brave, taste the suburbs of the 1960s.

Again, this seems all too culturally specific. I've never seen a 'Jell-O salad' outside of a lurid food photograph in an American cookbook, and if I ever encountered one in the real world I'd fall on it with gusto, but I know that many Americans see it as a grotesque suburban historical archetype.

And here's Partridge discussing *How to Keep Him (After You've Caught Him)* (1968):

Jinx Kragen and Judy Perry (the authors) approach their gendered food duties with humor and sophistication. This tour stop finds our authors in one of their suburban homes, playing hostesses to social hour with their fellow suburban wives and holding court with their witty observations about men. The snacks and cocktails served here are not the foods of the hour, but rather a discussion of the foods they should each be serving when the wives return to their own homesteads for the evening meal. Kragen and Perry have categorized all the different kinds of husbands a woman could have, and they champion cooking food specifically for individual types of husbands.

Kragen and Perry are unimpressed by husbands who won't try new and exciting foods, designating them as 'old Charlies'. Adventurous husbands relish culinary exotica such as curry soup (a can of cream-of-chicken soup with curry powder added) while old Charlies want meatloaf.

When I was growing up in the Sheffield suburbs, my own more or less suburban dad would have screamed the house down if my mother had served him either curried soup or meatloaf. Our suburban menu was heavy on pies (sweet and savoury), stews, a weekly roast, fish in milk, liver and onions, and so on. It was the way my father wanted it.

My mother could afford to be a little more experimental with me, sometimes serving 'convenience food', which seemed very modern. These foods included Vesta curries and chow mein, which at the time seemed rather good but would have been completely unacceptable to my dad. Fellow Sheffielder and stand-up comedian Graham Fellows (as John Shuttleworth) has got reams of material out of Vesta meals. And now that I think about it, I reckon my dad's objections to these fancy modern foods may have been that they were too suburban. Despite his slight move up in the world, he wanted to stick with the good working-class fare he was brought up on. It was only after he died that my mother was able to cook rice or pasta for herself. It should also be said that I never, ever saw her consult a cookbook

My parents rarely invited anybody round to their house to eat, and even then it was only very close family. It's often struck me that the food people eat at home under their own roof is a kind of family secret, not a dirty one but something very private. When you're a kid there's nothing weirder that going round to a friend or relative's house and finding they don't eat exactly the same things that you do. I discovered, for example, that my Auntie Daisy served bread and butter with tinned fruit. I thought that was wild. In my adolescence I once went to a posh girl's house (suburban to be sure, in Broomhill, Betjeman's lauded suburb) and found they were having whole baked onions with cheese sauce – it seemed as exotic as caviar, as California Dip.

If my parents weren't keen on having people round, they were even less keen on eating out. True there were fewer options back then, and money may have been tight, but it wasn't as though they sat around bemoaning the lack of good casual dining at a convenient suburban restaurant. They might have enjoyed the classlessness of an American diner, if there'd been any English equivalent, but there never really was; perhaps the Lyons' Corner House was as near as it got.

Diners started out in America before World War II as primarily urban, working-class places where men would eat on their way to work. Some were specifically Greek or Jewish or Italian. But as Greg Dickinson writes in *Suburban Dreams: Imagining and Building the Good Life* (2015), 'In the postwar world, diners repositioned themselves as more generically American and appealing to suburban family appetites through menu, architecture and marketing shifts, all of which deemphasized ethnic specificity and appealed to returning Victorian family values.' I'm not completely convinced that postwar America was awash with Victorian values, but OK, we'll let that go.

In a chapter headed 'The Return of Ethnicity and the Embodiment of Suburban Restaurants', Dickinson writes: 'While the immediate postwar suburban restaurant strove to empty its food and space of the localizing aesthetics of ethnicity, by the end of the twentieth century mass-produced chain-restaurant food returned to ethnicity with a vengeance.' By which he means that many an American suburb mall will these days be likely to include a Panda Express (Chinese), a Taco Bell (Mexican), an Olive Garden (Tuscan), and so on. These aren't so much faux as muted.

The late, blessed and much missed, food critic Jonathan Gold, the only food writer to win a Pulitzer Prize and the only Pulitzer Prize-winner with whom I've ever shared a pig's foot, once reviewed an Olive Garden for the *LA Weekly*. It was an April's Fool prank gone wrong. He concluded, 'I wondered how much straight Galliano would deliver me to a merciful death. I'm the snob. I will always be the snob.' Jonathan Gold was the least snobbish eater I've ever met but his review has deterred me from ever entering an Olive Garden, even though I'm sure I've eaten in much worse places.

Dickinson continues, 'The aestheticized ethnicity of the suburban restaurants responds directly to the problems of locating ourselves in time and place. Just as in late modernity it is difficult to locate ourselves in time so it is difficult to locate a natural body behind the technologies and cultures of the extended corpus.' Indeed, they talk of little else at the Meadowhall shopping mall in Sheffield, a place I know a little. But even there you can find a Thai restaurant, a sushi bar, a couple of Mexican restaurants (one of them a 'burrito bar'), Frankie & Benny's, which 'brings together the best of American and Italian', as well as what feels like the more 'local' Harvester and Nando's. There are also a number of places that started out as American franchises: KFC, McDonald's, TGI Fridays and Subway. Does all this count as suburban food? Since it's in a suburban shopping centre I think we have to say yes. We're reaching a stage where a taco may be considered at least as suburban as a shepherd's pie.

Surprisingly, to me anyway, I've found quite a few restaurants around the world that have the word Suburban in their name; The Suburban Bar and Lounge in Wimbledon, Suburban Grill and Burgers in Coulsdon, Suburban Eats in Melville, New York, the Suburban Diner in Paramus New Jersey, the Suburban Café in Durban, South Arica, the Suburban Grille in Melbourne, Australia, the Suburban Restaurant in Kerali, India (it's in the 'Suburban Complex' at Palarivattom Junction). I'm sure there are many, many more.

It's not clear what the owners of these restaurants are trying to convey with those names: that the restaurant isn't too grand, the food not too challenging, not like one of those fancy urban or *metropolitan* restaurants? Perhaps. However, an online and entirely unscientific investigation of these restaurants' menus, and others, reveals a random and diverse notion of what suburban food might be. Pizzas and burgers feature strongly but not universally, and the Suburban Restaurant in Kerali in fact serves Chinese food. There is no obvious consensus or commonality. This is not so surprising. Nobody ever said that all suburbs were the same, so why should all suburban restaurant menus be?

And in any case where would these restaurateurs look for guidance with their menu? Jessica Partidge's cohort might be as good a place as any, because as far as I can tell there is no contemporary volume titled *Suburban Cookery*, *The Suburban Chef* or anything of that sort. I did find one of those spiral-bound. self-published, fund-raising American books titled *Suburban Cooking*, with recipes donated by members of the Suburban Christian Church of Corvallis, Oregon. The subtitle is, 'Taste and see that the Lord is good.' Other than that, nothing much.

There is a Facebook group titled The Suburban Cookbook, with recipes that include doughnuts, meatloaf, tacos, with a few reviews of ready meals, including a recent post about

Trader Joe's lamb vindaloo, which is described as 'spicy fun'. The group declares its mission is 'to defend the Suburbs to those who propagate the notion that there is some sort of stigma to suburban life.' Uphill work for sure where some are concerned, but perhaps easier when you have a curry in one hand and a doughnut in the other.

11

Pounding Down in Poundbury

If you want to see an architect grimace, and most of us aren't averse to seeing that, mention Poundbury. You don't have to say you like it or that you believe it's a good thing or that you're thinking of living there. Just saying the name is all it takes.

Poundbury was the brainchild and passion project of Prince Charles, built on land he owned via the Duchy of Cornwall in Dorset. It was founded in the mid-1990s and is still a work in progress. Much of the literature describes it as an 'urban extension' of Dorchester, which is a way of trying to say it's not a suburb, but who's going to believe that? A suburb is what a suburb does. The writer and curator Stephen Bayley, clearly not a fan, described Poundbury as a 'sterile, suffocating dormitory town'. Or a suburb. Bayley is not an architect though he is an

honorary fellow of the Royal Institute of British Architects, and
so he grimaces along with the rest of them. Naturally I had to
go to Poundbury on a field trip.

Here's a question, and maybe it's a thought experiment: if by
some accident of wealth and birth you found yourself in a
position to create from scratch a brand new community/envi-
ronment/experiment in living, or indeed suburb, would you do
it? Well of course you would. We're all utopians to some degree
and the opportunity of making a place in your own image, a
place that conformed to all your own specifications, rules and
prejudices, would be irresistible, wouldn't it?

And the next question, if you thought this new place needed a
town square, and that's not an unreasonable thing to think, might
you also think it needed a big statue right there in the middle
of it? If so, maybe you'd choose something solid but modern
and challenging, not Damien Hirst but perhaps something by
Anthony Gormley or Rachel Whiteread, or if you wanted to
go more old school you might go for a Barbara Hepworth or a
Henry Moore.

Or possibly you'd want to go even more old school and
commission a statue of a figure from history or mythology:
Boudicca, Apollo, Sappho, that kind of thing. I know that it
wouldn't be an easy choice, but I'd like to suggest that however
long you thought about it, it would be a very cold day in Dorset
before you thought, 'What the inhabitants of this new utopia of
mine really need is a stonking great statue of my late grandma!'

But if you were Prince Charles you would, it appears, decide
that a larger than life-size statue of your nan, Elizabeth the Queen
Mother, would fit the bill just perfectly. Would it bother you that
at most times of the day there'd be a pigeon sitting on the old
lady's plumed hat, and that from time this bird, or one very like
it, would excrete on her head and face? I think it would bother
me, but the evidence is that it didn't bother Charles.

The statue is in Queen Mother Square. Nearby is a pub, designed by Quinlan and Francis Terry, named after Prince Charles's wife – the Duchess of Cornwall Inn, an odd choice of name it seems to me, although I know there are plenty of pubs named the Prince of Wales. And just across the way, opposite the Waitrose, is a block of luxury flats that looks, deliberately, like a faux Buckingham Palace.

Incidentally, there is no grass in this public square, no benches, no identifiable pavements, no fences for that matter: it's not a place for hanging around. There is also very little separation between pedestrians and cars, though there are some bollards protecting the statue. They might also in some circumstances protect pedestrians, but that's obviously not their prime reason for existing. As a walker you're free to stroll across Queen Mother Square but it's best to keep your eye open for cars coming out of nowhere.

This lack of pedestrian friendliness comes as a surprise. Poundbury was supposedly built to be a super-pedestrian-friendly place. The Prince would have you believe he's a great advocate of walking. In 2004, he set down his ten design principles for places to live. Number five asks for

> The creation of well-designed enclosures. Rather than clusters of separate houses set at jagged angles, spaces that are bounded and enclosed by buildings are not only more visually satisfying, they encourage walking and feel safer.

An anecdotal aside here: back in the day, an old friend of mine attended Cambridge University at the same time as Prince Charles. The friend was walking home late one night through the empty and occasionally malevolent streets of the centre of Cambridge: town and gown relations weren't completely harmonious at the time, and the friend saw Prince Charles some distance away, walking towards him, their paths destined to cross.

When they got close enough, they made brief eye contact and the Prince gave a little shrug and a backwards turn of the head that my friend interpreted as meaning, 'Look what I have to put up with.' There, walking twenty yards or so behind Charles, was a bodyguard, whom we assume was always with him. These days he surely has more than one. So I suspect the Prince has rarely if ever felt unprotected while walking, though that probably isn't the same as feeling safe. No doubt anxieties about kidnapping and assassination never quite go away when he's in public.

Given those circumstances, Charles's taste for bounded spaces isn't wholly unreasonable or surprising, and it's certainly shared by Leon Krier, his co-conspirator in urban design, the man appointed by the Prince in 1988 to plan Poundbury. Krier, born in Luxemburg, is as much architectural theorist as architect, a man apparently better at creating manifestos than buildings, a man with a portfolio of unrealised projects, though he did get to design the base on which the Queen Mum statue sits. And presumably he's one architect who doesn't grimace at the mere mention of Poundbury.

In his writings and lectures, Krier denounces Modernism, the ubiquity of the car and of course suburbia. He's against skyscrapers, which is also to say he's against lifts or elevators, and reckons you should be able to get to the top floor of any building by walking up the stairs, of which there should never be more than a hundred. Has he ever lived in a building that required him to walk up a hundred stairs on a daily basis? Has he ever tried to move furniture up or down a hundred stairs? Somehow I doubt it. Krier also posits a city made up of quarters or quadrants, each of no more that 80 acres, the centres of which (however we define centre in this case) can be crossed in the course of a ten-minute walk, which frankly sounds like a rather parochial environment.

He's also against zoning, believing that places of work, residence and leisure should all be located close together, with citizens able to walk from one to the other. Now, this sounds perfectly sensible – Frank Lloyd Wright is just one architect who had similar thoughts, and it pretty much describes Hillsborough, the 'suburb' in Sheffield where I was born and where my mother's side of the family lived for most of their lives. Factories, steelworks, pubs, shops, a dog track and a football ground were all walking distance from each other. But I'm pretty sure that this rough, industrial, sometimes grubby and down-at-heel, working-class enclave of Sheffield would not have been Krier's urban dream, much less Prince Charles's.

Poundbury strives to be an anti-suburb. The biggest buildings there are much grander, the architectural styles more diverse, than you'd find in most suburbs. The place is very clean, the buildings look fresh out of the box, although they inevitably lack patina; how could they not given their lack of age? Semi-detached houses are few in number, so for that matter are front gardens, which if they do exist are very small. And unlike Hampstead Garden Suburb, there are plenty of garden walls, most of them at least head height so there's no peering into anybody's back garden.

However, Poundbury is *not* an anti-suburb. Part of what makes it essentially suburban is its proximity to Dorchester. That's where the two railway stations are, that's where the cinema and the bookshop and the museums and the interesting restaurants are. These things are absent from Poundbury, but Dorchester is close enough that if you want those things (and admittedly not everyone in Poundbury does) you can easily drive there or hop on an electric bus and go into town. You could even walk there at a pinch. To that extent, Poundbury functions just like a suburb of Dorchester.

You do feel perfectly safe walking around, and yet despite Charles's and Krier's preferences there are a good few alleys: that tends to go with having high garden walls. In 2009 the *Guardian* managed to find a single mother of three who hated the alleys of

Poundbury. She was quoted as saying, 'I find them really scary and dangerous. They're great in the day but at night the kids come and bang on the door and then run off down them. I'm frightened to walk them by myself at night.'

The *Guardian* article (by Steven Morris and Robert Booth) continues, 'She darts back into her house as a group of young men with a box of beer walks past on the way to the park.' No doubt having random youths banging on your door at night is very unpleasant, but you could also argue that people who feel the need to dart inside their home at the mere sight of young men carrying a box of beer don't know when they're well off. Or perhaps she was just darting inside because she'd had enough of talking to journalists. Those same reporters also found people unhappy with the quality of some of the Poundbury homes. People pay over the odds to live there and expect a great deal, but in fact there are teething problems with cracks and water leaks here just as in any new-build.

Of course you don't get to see the water leaks when you're just walking the streets. You see the cleanliness, the tidiness, and no more than the occasional small expanse of weather-stained rendering. (There's the patina we were missing.) To be fair there were a good few people walking around, quite a few of them with dogs of course. There were a few cats, walking by themselves. There were people going to and from the shops on foot – I saw a woman with a big High Grove shopping bag – though the serious shoppers of course had their cars. In fact the place is amazingly car-friendly, perhaps because, at the moment, there's a great deal of free parking. However, since the population of Poundbury is scheduled to double in the next few years, a parking spot adjacent to the Duchess of Cornwall Inn may become increasingly hard to find.

There are, naturally, some rules and regulations that have to be obeyed if you want to live in Poundbury. Some seem more or less reasonable: no chopping down of trees, no building of extra fences and walls, no alterations or extensions without permission; but the rule about no parking of caravans or boats in gardens or parking spaces seems a bit less reasonable. An Englishman's back garden may not be his country estate but it's surely a place where he can put his caravan. Another rule runs – 'no signboard advertisement placard or house name to be placed in the window of any house or on the exterior without approval of the Prince'. Not even a house name? That seems a bit much, and I did in fact see a house with a wooden plaque declaring it to be named El Sidewinder, but had it been considered and approved by the Prince? I'd be amused and delighted to think so.

There are also rules about what colours you're allowed to paint the exterior of your property, though that's pretty standard in conservation areas. Even so I'd been wandering around for quite a while before I considered the domestic garages of Poundbury. There are a lot of them, many in blocks and not immediately adjacent to the homes of the car owners, and there seemed to be a surprising number of flats located above what were clearly other people's garages, which surely comes with all kinds of problems and annoyances from rumbling car engines and the opening and closing of garage doors at all times of the day and night; or possibly the inhabitants of Poundbury are amazingly considerate and quiet.

It was notable, that with a very few exceptions, the vast majority of these garage doors were painted plain black. Now, I'm not suggesting that selecting the paint colour for your garage door is an inalienable freedom or a great opportunity for self-realisation, but my own feeling is that I'd prefer my garage door to be any colour as long as it wasn't black. I also thought those plain black 'canvases' might represent a challenge and a provocation to the street-artist youth of Poundbury, but apparently not, and that may be because in Poundbury the youth is in short supply, or maybe it's just corralled in the 'wrong' part of town.

The only graffiti I saw in the whole place was on the walls of a faux classical temple, actually an electricity sub-station, right by the sports ground. It was also, coincidentally or not, right by the council estate, which I eventually wandered into, and which is outside Poundbury proper.

I've discussed elsewhere the extent to which a council estate is or isn't a form of suburbia, and in this case it certainly looked and felt suburban enough, though quite different from anywhere I'd been before on that day. And the houses here had certain things that Poundbury houses didn't have; substantial front gardens for a start. Some of them, as ever, had been paved over to accommodate a car, some were meticulously well-tended, though some were seriously neglected and filled with builders' rubbish, and although not many of the houses had a garage, the few that did had doors that were painted in many different colours. There were also people on the streets, some of them mooching, some of them working on the houses, some of them giving me funny looks. There was a feeling of rough, striving humanity, which there sure as hell wasn't in Poundbury proper.

But the best thing of all, which made the visit entirely worthwhile, was a sign resting on a dead bush in somebody's front garden. It would not of course have been allowed in Poundbury, but in the suburbs it's not all that unusual to see a self-employed sole trader, a painter or decorator or plumber, put up a sign in his own garden advertising his services, but never before had I seen a garden sign like the one I saw here – a pink background and in chunky, blue letters with a drop shadow, the single word TATTOO and then a phone number, which was not quite legible. It almost made you want to get a tattoo. I returned to the main part of Poundbury. It wasn't a shock to the system, more a gentle reconfiguring of the brain waves, a quietening, a powering-down.

Not long after I'd completed my field trip, I saw a headline blazing out from the *Daily Telegraph* which read, 'Vandals turn Prince Charles's dream village of Poundbury into "Ugly Buildings."' Those quotation marks were a clue that this wasn't simple vandalism, and having read the article I thought the word 'vandals' in that headline might also have been in quotation marks.

The story was about some local wag or wags or possibly bricolagists who'd manipulated a road sign that directed traffic into Poundbury from a local roundabout on the A35. They'd covered over the name Poundbury with an official-looking sign, same font, slightly smaller font size, and on this new sign it said 'Ugly buildings.' A close look would tell you it was a fake, but you don't get a close look when you're in your car rapidly approaching a roundabout on the A35.

I think there are worse ways of describing Poundbury than as the home of 'ugly buildings', and more accurate ways too. I didn't find them ugly, just a bit dull, and you may say well, what else do you expect in suburbia? Also a bit pretentious, which you don't expect in suburbia. However, Margaret Morrisey of the Poundbury Residents' Association was not amused by the manipulated sign and was quoted as saying, 'If you don't like it there's no need to be rude,' which is true as far as it goes, although wouldn't it have been better to say, 'There aren't any ugly buildings here.' Maybe she thought that wasn't strictly true.

Poundbury gets compared to Disneyland and Stepford (where the wives come from), and the sense of a stage or movie set is hard to shake. There's a lack of substance, a lack of depth. But perhaps an equally good comparison might be Ruritania, the invention of novelist Anthony Hope, the country that appears in *The Prisoner of Zenda* and *Rupert of Hentzau*, which was obviously not by any means suburban, but it was a two-dimensional confection, a stage set on which improbable romances could unfold, the fiefdom of a frustrated heir to the throne who had grown tired of waiting for the crown and had decided to create his own little kingdom, a place that he could rule, albeit rather distantly. Needless to say, neither the Prince of Wales nor Leon Krier lives in Poundbury. Krier spends much of his time when not on the international architectural-lecture circuit, in the South of France. Prince Charles, of course, has many homes, including a 'private nature retreat' in Transylvania. Really.

In the end, how did I feel about Poundbury? Well I didn't like it all that much, not because it was too suburban (the problem that a lot of people have with it) but because I wished it would accept its suburbanity with a little more grace and honesty. I found it faux and affected, and I think I might have enjoyed it a lot more if it had been called Windsor Garden Suburb. Even so I won't in the future grimace at the mere mention of its name.

Beyond Disneyland, Stepford and Ruritania, the more I think about it the more I'm reminded of The Village in the TV series *The Prisoner,* a place so calm and tranquil and well-ordered that you suspect something absolutely terrible could happen at any moment, even if it doesn't. 'Questions are a burden to others. Answers are a prison for oneself.'

The Prisoner was filmed in the real-life Portmeirion in Wales, designed by Clough Williams-Ellis, which conjures the atmosphere of the fictional place within the show, The Village. And how would Clough Williams-Ellis have felt about Poundbury? We don't know exactly, but we can perhaps glean a few clues from his book, said to be largely written by his wife Amabel, who was part of the Strachey family, titled *England and the Octopus* (1928). The octopus was, need I say, suburbia.

12

Suburban Screens

When I started thinking about movies set in suburbia, three came immediately to mind: *Edward Scissorhands* (1990), *American Beauty* (1999) and *A Serious Man* (2009). All of them assert that living in suburbia is a difficult business, involving a considerable degree of suffering. I saw them in cinemas when they were first released, and liked them all very much. I've seen reruns over the years, and of course I watched them again, along with many others, before writing this chapter. Our feelings about movies change over the years, and certainly our feelings about the actors in them change too, and I realise that the feelings we have about the stars of the first two of those movies have changed in quite unexpected ways in recent times.

There's a moment at the end of *American Beauty* when Angela and Jane, two teenage schoolgirls who are destined not to have a long-lasting friendship, argue with each other. Angela, the sexy, supposedly exotic, knowing and experienced girl with model good looks (Mina Suvari) denounces Jane (Thora Birch) for being a freak. Jane doesn't regard this as much of an insult, but she counters by saying, 'You'll never be a freak because you're just too perfect.' Angela says, 'Well at least I'm not ugly,' and Jane's boyfriend pitches in and says, 'Yes, you are. And you're boring. And you're totally ordinary. And you know it.'

Being a freak or a bore: are those really the only two options open to suburbanites? Maybe. *American Beauty* is largely about a character who has become bored with himself, and becomes increasingly freakish. That character is Lester Burnham (played by Kevin Spacey). He and his wife Carolyn (Annette Benning) and daughter Jane live in a very pleasant house – white picket fence, roses (Carolyn is a rose-grower) – in a very pleasant suburb, rather ritzier than you imagine any real-life Burnhams could afford on their salaries. She's a not very successful realtor, he does something nebulous in 'magazines'.

We're given our aerial overview of the suburb: a familiar trope in suburban movies. Filming was done in various not easily recognisable, and not geographically adjacent, Los Angeles locations. And as the camera passes over houses and trees we first hear Lester's voice over, speaking from the dead as it happens, just like in *Sunset Boulevard*, telling us that he felt dead even when he was alive. Later, before he's dead, as it were, he says he feels sedated, and later still that he's been in a coma for twenty years and now he's waking up.

Waking up turns out to be a long, slow, painful process. Lester sabotages his chances of keeping his job, buys a Trans Am, smokes dope, and lusts after Angela, his daughter's friend. Angela appears keen enough to have sex with Lester, and he looks fanciable enough. We see him getting fit, running, developing muscles, and we, and others, see him naked in his garage, working out.

Staring out of the window to see what the neighbours are up to is standard behaviour in any suburb but here the boy next door, Ricky Fitts, a self-confessed weirdo, part of the family that's just moved in – ex-military father, a former colonel, and his utterly inert, possibly medicated, wife – doesn't just *look*, he *videos* what he sees. Much of Ricky's video footage features Jane, who eventually comes to find him and his activities charming, but he's prepared to film anything, including Lester working out.

The father also looks out of his window and sees his son in the garage next door with Lester, and thinks the boy's giving Lester a blowjob, because that's the kind of thing he thinks about a lot. But we the audience know that the boy isn't doing anything sexual with Lester, he's just his drug supplier.

Lester's wife Carolyn is really pretty dreadful: brittle, phony, narrowly aspirational, telling her daughter she should be grateful for what she's got; when she was growing up 'we didn't even have our own home'. She had to live in a rented duplex. Lester tells us she wasn't always like this, which leaves you wondering how much of a role he played in her unfortunate transformation. Certainly he drives her into the arms of another man, who encourages her to learn how to use a gun. We suspect early on that something terrible is going to happen.

When Lester attempts a jokey, ironic seduction of his wife, and is in some danger of spilling beer on their $4000 Italian silk sofa, she understandably points this out to him and he says, 'This isn't life, this is just stuff.' Don't you love it when Hollywood goes antimaterialist? Clearly it *is* just stuff but it's stuff they've worked for and paid for, and I'd say that if by some chance you happen to own a $4000 couch, it's probably better not to spill beer on it. Is that too suburban of me? But did Lester agree to the purchase? Did he help select it? Did he used to like the couch and then fell out of love with it? Or did he only have it in the house to placate Carolyn? We never find out.

He says the marriage 'is a commercial for how normal we are', but given his increasing cynicism and alienation it seems to be a commercial for something quite different, perhaps for lack of attachment. Lester's angst is real but there's something very exhibitionistic about it. He doesn't just quit his job, he insults his boss and blackmails a different superior, successfully, it appears. And he doesn't just go and look for another job, he takes the first and worst job he can find, working in a fast-food joint. As for his relationship skills, never does he have a conversation with his wife about what's wrong with their marriage, or how they might improve their lives; he just insults her. Yes, Lester is funny, clever and sarcastic (and OK, occasionally a bit camp), but that surely means he'd be infuriating and intolerable to live with. A wife might very well think about killing him, if somebody else didn't kill him first.

Lester gets ever more disengaged as the movie progresses. At the end when he's at his most detached, with his job, marriage and family in ruins, after he's turned down the opportunity to have sex with Angela, an urge that's obsessed him throughout the movie, because he discovers she's a virgin, he says he feels great. He's now totally free of attachment, and then he's shot dead by his closeted, ex-military neighbour, which arguably makes him freer still.

The neighbour has just made a pass at him, and his rejection of the colonel may not be proof positive of Lester's heterosexuality, but there's no sense in the movie that he's struggling with his sexuality. And in fact he handles the unwanted gay approach very well. He gives the colonel a manly hug and says, 'You got the wrong idea.' It seems the right thing to do, but the fact that the rejected neighbour then shoots Lester in the head may suggest that some things in life can't be dealt with by being detached.

There may be an overarching, if not an especially original, argument in the film in favour of being yourself and not living a lie. Carolyn Burnham does seem to be a phoney, Angela plays at being a sex kitten but is in fact a lost little suburban schoolgirl. The colonel's misunderstanding of his own and other people's sexuality is, of course, a lie or self-deception of a much higher order. But when Lester is being droll, cruel, bitter, aggressive, vicious, he's being totally himself.

Is it a movie about the stifling horrors of suburbia? Well, Lester isn't happy there but he never contemplates going any-where else. Within the terms of the movie, going elsewhere is not offered as much of a solution for him, though the young folk – Jane Burnham and Ricky Fitts – do seem to be about to run away to New York together. After being a successful drug dealer in the suburbs Ricky is ready to try his hand at being a drug dealer in the Big Apple. Hard to imagine what could go wrong with *that* plan.

There was a feeling among certain commentators, and among people I knew, some gay, some not, that this was Kevin Spacey's coded 'coming out movie' or perhaps they thought it *ought* to have been. Nobody seemed to have any doubt that Spacey was gay. But if it's *coded* it's not really coming out, is it? In fact, at the time, it could have been regarded as Spacey's 'staying in movie'. But then circumstances meant that Spacey was outed whether he wanted to be or not. He faced a barrage of sexual assault charges, in the UK and the US, although none of them was proven and none of the investigations are currently open.

So how do we feel about Kevin Spacey now, and more importantly, how do we feel about *American Beauty*? The movie's screenwriter Alan Ball has said he thinks the movie is 'tainted' by Spacey's presence, and I can see you might be dismayed if your best-known screenplay was tarred with the Spacey brush. Do I have sympathy for the young men who were groped against their will by Spacey? Naturally I do. But is it some moral failing in me that I can still watch the film and find Spacey a believable, if actorly, larger than life, suburban husband and father. You'll no doubt be able to make up your mind on that one. Do I still think *American Beauty* is a pretty good film about suffering in suburbia? Yes.

*

If you want to see somebody suffering in suburbia, and suffering beautifully, take a look at *Edward Scissorhands* (1990), directed by Tim Burton, starring Johnny Depp. Initially Edward lives in a threateningly spooky, ruined Gothic mansion up on the hill, but it's right at the end of a suburban street, well within walking distance of the nearest houses.

Edward has lived in the mansion since he was 'born', or 'created', or whatever it was, by the Inventor, a doddery Vincent Price (in his last performance). Life looks a bit rough up there in the mansion but Edward has solitude and tranquillity which is only broken by the arrival of a perky Avon lady (Peg Boggs, played by Dianne Wiest) who's finding it hard to sell cosmetics to her more immediate suburban neighbours and in desperation tries to sell farther afield. She finds Edward up in the mansion looking a terrified and damaged mess, and invites him home to live with her and her family.

Now, obviously we all know that the movie is a fantasy, and I'm perfectly prepared to suspend disbelief, and accept that Peg Boggs might be the kind of saintly woman who takes pity on waifs and strays and brings them into the family home. What I find harder to believe, even within the terms of the fantasy, is that she's the first person ever to venture up to the mansion on the hill. If we know anything about suburban housewives, whether in general or specifically the ones in this movie, it's that they're an inquisitive bunch. Wouldn't a couple of them have decided, perhaps after a couple of early-evening martinis, to go up there and have a nose around?

And how about the young uns? Again, life and cinema have taught us that suburban youth can't resist a ruin. That mansion would be a perfect place for hanging out, making out, drinking beer and smoking dope. Not in the Edward Scissorhands universe, however. And while we're being sceptical and literal, why for the love of God, did the Inventor give Edward scissors for hands in the first place? We learn that he had plans to replace the blades with wax manikin-style hands, but as a first version, wouldn't just about anything have been better than scissors?

On a more positive note, the suburb Edward Scissorhands moves to looks thoroughly enticing. Again we're introduced to it via a moving aerial shot, but here the houses are painted in wonderful ice-cream colours. They look neat, orderly and fantastic in at least two senses. As Peg Boggs drives Edward through this suburban wonderland for the first time, he's filled with awe at what he sees, and she says to him, playing it absolutely straight, 'You have every reason to be excited,' and the truth is yes, he does, and he's equally excited by suburban interiors and furnishings.

Much of the movie was filmed at Tinsmith Circle in Lutz, Florida.* There's a website that compares the suburb as it was in the movie with the way it looks now. Apart from a change of paint colours and the fact that the greenery has shot up over the last thirty years, it still looks very similar.

As Edward tries to settle in to suburbia, he's understandably confused by the basic rules and rituals: the classic cinematic fish out of water. But because of his skills as a topiarist, then as a trimmer of dog fur and, eventually, as a cutter of women's hair, he's accepted by the locals, especially the women. He's a subject of curiosity and fascination, much of it sexual. The neighbourhood wives vie for his attention and approval, sometimes using food as a means of seduction. There's a sexy neighbour (Kathy Baker as Joyce) who tries to turn his head with ambrosia salad: a kind of a fruit salad, capable of enormous variation but usually made with canned fruit – mandarin oranges, pineapple, cherries – along with mini marshmallows, the whole thing bound together with some kind of dairy product, such as whipped cream, sour cream,

---

*   I once went to Lutz to interview some people who lived full-time in a gated clothing-optional swingers resort. It was as suburban as could be, though it was gated and the armed guard on the gate appeared to take his duties very seriously. Nobody would be satisfying their curiosity by wandering in there on a field trip, uninvited.

yoghurt or cottage cheese. I suspect that few people even in the American suburbs eat this 'unironically' any more.

Joyce also tries to seduce Edward, in her case more directly by getting naked in the back room of an empty hair salon in the local mall. This is just one more thing Edward doesn't understand, and possibly the sequence is supposed to mark his loss of innocence.

From then on things start to go wrong for him. The bad local youth get him involved with a robbery, though he's only doing it because he's besotted with Kim Boggs (played by Wynona Rider) and he thinks it will make her happy. When he's caught mid-theft, the neighbourhood's perception of him changes abruptly. He saves a child from being run down by a van, which you'd think might redeem him, but in the process he scratches up the kid's face with his scissor hands. The quirky and charming outsider has become a freak and a monster. The final scenes of the movie echo *Frankenstein* with an angry mob baying for Edward's blood. In the end he kills his chief tormentor and returns to the ruined mansion, the suburbanites believing him to be dead, largely thanks to the help of a sympathetic Black cop – not an inhabitant of the suburb, we can be pretty certain.

I don't know that there's any hard and fast lesson to be drawn from this, but if there is, it could be that suburbia will accept a certain degree of weirdness but only so much, and its inhabitants are always ready to turn against you if you're *too* different, and especially if you commit a crime. The police's opinion that Edward is so adrift in his newfound world that he doesn't even know what the rules are, doesn't seem to count for much. Or is the meaning simply that freaks such as Edward are better off living in Gothic mansions than in the Florida suburbs? I don't know if that's what Tim Burton intended, and I'm not sure it's true. It might be nice to think that the moral is simply that we're all freaks, whether in suburbia or not, but the movie doesn't quite support this. There's nothing at all freakish about the Winona

Ryder character, for instance. She seems utterly normal, squeaky clean and really rather dull, and yet Edward sees in her a kindred soul. Could this be read as an indication that being a freak and being dull might ultimately amount to much the same thing?

So how do we feel about Johnny Depp now, and more importantly, how do we feel about *Edward Scissorhands*? Only recently has Depp brought and lost his libel suit against the *Sun* newspaper, during which an English judge declared him to be a wife-beater. Does the court case change how we feel about Johnny Depp? Well yes, I think it does. We already knew, from extant accounts published long before the court appearance, that he was a movie star on the receiving end of more money, drugs and sex than most of us can begin to imagine. Even so the home life of our own dear Johnny did come as a shock – the violence, the blood, the broken glass, the bruises, the alleged threats.

It's a peculiar kind of relief to turn to *A Serious Man*, directed by Joel and Ethan Coen, starring Michael Stuhlbarg, a man who as far as we can tell has led a blameless life. The movie tells the story of Larry Gopnik, a physics professor living in an unnamed suburb of Minneapolis, in 1967. It was filmed in Bloomington, and photographs of the place, taken in the 1950s and '60s by Irwin Denison Norling are collected in the book *Suburban World: The Norling Photographs*, is cited as a visual inspiration for the film, but it seems a rather distant inspiration to me. The film establishes its sixties' credentials more directly with a soundtrack that features an awful lot of Jefferson Airplane, although it also includes Hendrix's *Machine Gun*, which by all accounts wasn't played live until 1969, and wasn't recorded till 1970. Still, a soundtrack doesn't have to stick rigidly to period authenticity.

There's also plenty of Jewish music on the soundtrack, and the world depicted in the movie is primarily Jewish, which may be surprising given some of the received wisdom about the ethnic composition of the suburbs. This Minneapolis version is not an exclusively Jewish enclave, but only one Gentile neighbour figures and he's a gun-toting redneck who's building a boathouse (yes, in a suburban subdivision) that is encroaching on Larry's property line. He's dismissed by another neighbour in a single, simple comic put down: 'A goy!' and that explains everything.

Larry also has to deal with a couple of South Koreans, father and son, who try to bribe him (successfully in the end) into giving the son a passing grade in the exams he's just failed. There are also a few cops and secretaries who may well not be Jewish but they hardly make any impression compared with the characters who are: the doctor, the lawyers, the rabbis.

The scene that had stayed most firmly in my mind, prior to reacquainting myself with the movie, and which seemed to confirm the film as an archetypal suburban saga, comes after about half an hour when Larry climbs up onto the roof of his house to adjust his TV aerial. From up there he and the audience can look out across the suburb at all the other one-storey houses and feel above it all. It's a great and for me unforgettable image of a certain kind of American suburbia. The view is not exactly visually exciting but to an English eye it seems downright exotic: the absence of pavements, the sixties' cars, the gardens that are just unfenced expanses of grass, the unfinished look of the whole thing.

Larry can also see into the garden of his sexy female neighbour, one Mrs Samsky (played by Amy Landecke), who is 'enjoying the new freedoms'; her husband travels a lot, and, as Larry discovers, she has a good supply of marijuana, some of which she shares with him. Larry first sees her from on high, she's sunbathing nude behind the white fence of her house. This unsettles him, and causes him to lose his footing for a moment. A better, more sensible, man might not take advantage of this viewpoint, might not peep at his naked neighbour, but Larry can't resist. Worse and cruder directors than the Coens would probably have him fall off the roof, but very wisely they don't.

So far so suburban, and some of Larry's problems are thoroughly suburban: children who don't respect him and a brother who sleeps on the couch and shows no sign of getting a place of his own, though he does manage to get himself arrested for sodomy. And Larry's most pressing problem is his wife, who's found somebody she likes better and therefore kicks him out of the house so that he ends up living in a motel; and she also cleans out their joint bank account.

But some of his problems seem rather different from those normally encountered in suburbia. It's not every suburbanite who teaches physics at college level, and although people in suburbia worry about their work, he worries about getting academic tenure, which again is not *per se* one of the problems afflicting most inhabitants of suburbia. And it's certainly not every suburbanite, even if they're Jewish, who consults rabbis in an attempt to understand his own suffering, or tries to understand his suffering at all. For that matter, quite a lot of the action of the movie doesn't take place in the suburbs, rather it takes place in the synagogue, in a school, in Larry's own office and lecture theatre and in a doctor's office, as well as in the offices of the various lawyers Larry consults.

Much has been made of the suggestion that *A Serious Man* is a sixties' rendering of the Book of Job; I think Roger Ebert was the first to float this idea, though the Coen Brothers say that wasn't what they had in mind. Certainly Larry suffers, but don't the central characters in most movies suffer? If you ever sit in an office with a movie producer, he or she will certainly tell you how important it is that the protagonist be *in jeopardy*. Characters need to have problems to solve, whether it's how to save the world, or how to avoid killing your father and sleeping with your mother. Larry is ineffectual, but it doesn't rise to the level of Greek tragedy, and it hardly represents a fatal flaw. Therefore his problem within a problem is that he doesn't understand *why* bad things keep happening to him when he's done nothing to deserve it, and even at the end of the film, when it looks as though the worst of his problems may be over, there are suddenly some brand new ones: a tornado is about to hit the suburb, and Larry's doctor has found something ominous on his X-ray.

So I find myself debating whether or not *A Serious Man* is actually a movie *about* the suburbs, or just a movie set in the suburbs that might be set anywhere, addressing universal issues about the nature of suffering that are by no means only suburban. I realise that makes the film sound a bit dull and worthy, but of course it's neither of those things. One way of squaring the circle might be to say that universal issues apply in suburbia just as much as they apply anywhere else, and that Larry's fundamental question, 'Why are these terrible things happening to me?' is not satisfactorily answered either by the Coen Brothers, who don't even try to answer it, or by the Book of Job, which does.

Michael Stuhlbarg may have led a blameless life, but the fallout from the Kevin Spacey affair affected him directly. He was cast in a biopic of Gore Vidal, to play Howard Austen, Vidal's long-term companion. I'd have liked to see that. As far as I can tell, the film was completed, but the chances of its being released remain low.

You will have noticed, of course, that all three of the films on my shortlist are essentially, perhaps quintessentially, American (this despite Sam Mendes, the director of *American Beauty*, being English), and it gives me no pleasure to say this, but for some reason or other there are no great movies about British suburbia.

It's easy to think of truckloads of pretty good American suburban movies: *Blue Velvet*, *The Truman Show*, *Suburbicon*, *The Burbs* (with Tom Hanks, a particular favourite of mine), *The Whole Nine Yards* (ditto), *ET*, *Donny Darko*, the two versions of *The Stepford Wives*, and then at least two movies called simply *Suburbia*. Lots of horror movies: *Invasion of the Body Snatchers*, *Poltergeist*, *Halloween*, and a recent obscure, low-budget gem, *Garden Party Massacre*, containing some snappy lines such as,

'What did he do to Melanie? Where did he get a pickaxe in suburbia.'

And what does the British film industry have to offer? I consulted various real-world and online resources that recommended some 'great British suburban films'. These recommendations included *Bend it Like Beckham*, *Shaun of the Dead*, *Metroland*, *My Beautiful Laundrette*, various Carry On films, even *Confessions of a Window Cleaner*, but all in all I thought it was slim pickings.

One of the films that kept popping up in this context, and which I'd never heard of, was *Home at Seven* (1952), directed by and starring Ralph Richardson, based on a play by R.C. Sherriff, and the film doesn't do much to disguise its stage-bound origins.

The film's premise is terrific. It's about a commuter named David Preston (played by Richardson) who travels daily from his home in Bromley to Cannon Street, where he works in a bank, then in the evening he returns, always arriving home at seven. One night he gets back as usual, or so he believes, only to discover that it's not the day he thinks it is but a day later. He's arriving home twenty-four hours later than he thinks he is, and he has no memory of the missing day, thus playing with the idea that every day is pretty much identical for the suburban commuter.

This gap in his memory obviously disturbs him, the more so when he learns that during this blank period a considerable amount of money has gone missing from the Social Club, of which he's treasurer. Things get even worse when it turns out the club steward has been murdered.

Also Preston has a secret. It takes him an hour to get home every day, and his wife assumes he leaves work at six, but no, during the war he developed a small sherry habit. In fact he finishes work at five and every day slips into a pub called the Feathers for a couple of drinks, 'two was my limit,' before heading home. His wife Janet (Margaret Leighton) doesn't notice the sherry on his breath but then she may be distracted by her gardening – she has a magnificent display of Japanese chrysanthemums which play a modest role in the plot development – and she also does the cooking. 'You always knew the way to make toast,' says hubby.

Well, needless to say, further complications ensue, and at some point Preston becomes convinced that he actually did commit the murder on the missing day, although it seemed to me the movie got slightly less intriguing the longer it went on. I was expecting a twist that never came, and a *dea ex machina* suddenly pops up and saves the day, but it's fun while it lasts. And it is genuinely about suburban life, offering the possibility that murder and mayhem can happen even in the suburbs.

Finally, we can't discuss depictions of English suburbia without some mention of *Abigail's Party* (1977), 'devised' by Mike Leigh, starring Alison Steadman, a made-for-TV movie, before the term was current. It started life as a play at the Hampstead Theatre Club, that bastion of wholesome suburban values (that's irony), but gained a mass audience when it was broadcast by BBC television. On the box of my DVD copy it says, 'Shown on *Play for Today* in 1977, this "cocktail party from hell" wickedly took apart the tastelessness, pretensions and pomposity of England's aspiring suburban classes.' Well, where to start with that?

Perhaps with the fact that it doesn't depict a cocktail party from hell or from anywhere else because it doesn't depict a cocktail party at all, unless you think gin and tonic or Bacardi and coke are cocktails, and if you think that, you're wrong. At best it's a drinks party, or in fact just five people sitting about, drinking and talking, which describes a great many English plays from the 1970s.

So the event, or party, we're seeing is not Abigail's: Abigail is a kind of off-screen fifteen-year-old female Godot. Her mother Sue who is posh, and in fact totally unpretentious, though tightly wound, has come round for drinks with Beverley and Lawrence Moss, so that Abigail can have the house to herself for the party. Hard to imagine what could go wrong with *that* plan! There are noises off from the party all evening, and the audience anticipates disasters, but if they happen, we don't see them.

The action takes place entirely in the open-plan living room of the Mosses' house. Beverley is a former make-up demonstrator, Lawrence is an estate agent, and in his way he's every bit as phoney as Carolyn Burnham: Uriah Heep would think his telephone manner was a little too obsequious.

But the piece is all about Beverley. It's a virtuoso and 'look at me' part that certain actresses love to play, but it's also one of those parts that sucks all the air away from the other performers, so they just have to sit there and 'react'. Beverley is, no doubt about it, a monster, and the play sneers at her *passim* because of her suburban vulgarity. This includes, but is not limited to, putting red wine in the fridge, liking Demis Roussos, having strong opinions about lipstick, being enthusiastic about Majorca, serving crisps, nuts, and cheese and pineapple on sticks, and not liking olives. The posh neighbour Sue *does* like olives, and Lawrence claims to, but we're led to suspect that this may be a pretension.

In fact, the sneering shown towards Lawrence in *Abigail's Party* may be even greater than that shown towards Beverley. He's a bit of racist, complaining about the area becoming 'more mixed' – middle-class Sue has no problems with this, but worse are his cultural pretentions. He has a nicely bound set of the works of Shakespeare but doesn't or can't read them, and he likes 'light classical' music. He has a fondness for art – Van Gogh and Lowry are the examples we see – but the suggestion is that he likes them for the 'wrong' reasons. Beverley, inevitably, only likes erotic art. Anyway, spoiler alert, Lawrence has a heart attack and dies while listening to Beethoven's Fifth which he's put on as background music.

Unlike the poor scribe who wrote copy for the DVD box, I don't think *Abigail's Party* takes apart the tastelessness, pretensions and pomposity of England's aspiring suburban classes.

I think it demonstrates the pretensions, pomposity and con-descension of the English theatre-making classes. I accept that this may be a matter of hindsight. If I'd seen the play or the TV version in 1977 maybe I'd have thought that aspiring suburban-ites deserved all the scorn and abuse they got. My attitudes towards suburbia may have softened a little as time's gone by, but I think I'm an outlier in this. The stage version of *Abigail's Party* gets performed all over Britain all the time. It's a classic, a crowd pleaser, it puts bums on seats. It's regularly cited as a great piece of social satire. In Britain, snobbery, and sneering at imagined social 'inferiors', especially in suburbia, just never goes out of fashion.

13

Some Metropolitan Field Trips:
Saffron Park to Shangri-La

We could do worse than start this chapter with a quotation from Vincent Van Gogh, from a letter to his brother Theo, dated 7 October 1876, 'The suburbs of London have a peculiar charm, between the little houses and gardens there are open spots covered with grass and generally with a church or school or workhouse in the middle among the trees and shrubs. It can be so beautiful there when the sun is setting red in the evening mist.' London suburbs may have changed just a little since Van Gogh's day – those beautiful sunlit workhouses have gone for one thing – but even so …

I've tried to avoid making this book too London-centric, and I realise that I've probably failed. Since London is the British city with the largest population it's not surprising that it has the most suburbs. In further mitigation, I could also say that London is the city I know best and where I lived longest, in a lot of different locations, and we could debate how many and which ones were actually suburbs. Hendon? Yes. Stamford Hill (just like Ebenezer Howard)? Oh yes. Greenwich? Surely. Shepherd's Bush, maybe. East Ham, probably. Bloomsbury, I'd say not.

Peter Ackroyd in *London the Biography* (2000) writes, 'The suburbs are as old as the city itself; they were once the spillings and scourings of the city, unhappy and insalubrious … so that the area beyond the walls was in some way deemed threatening or lawless. It was neither city nor country; it represented London's abandoned trail across the earth.'

Historically, everything that wasn't in the City of London or the City of Westminster could once be considered a suburb, although that no longer seems a useful measure. Over time, outlying districts were incorporated into the city. Places such as Hackney or Bromley, even Chelsea, which were once no part of London became not only its suburbs, but part of the city itself. Again this confounds the idea that a suburb must be outside the *urbs*. Complicating matters further, today many places outside the city's actual boundaries still function as though they were London suburbs, the commuter belt and dormitory towns: Basildon, Berkhamstead, Beaconsfield, Banstead, Broxbourne, Bushey, and that's just a few of the Bs.

How many suburbs does London have? It's a good question, but if anybody knows the answer they're keeping it to themselves, possibly because they don't want to get into the business of defining a suburb. *London Suburbs* (1999), a good book by Andrew Saint et al, contains a gazetteer which you'd think would be a help in ascertaining the number, but it comes with the warning:

This gazetteer does not claim to be comprehensive; rather, it includes developments, groups of buildings, or, in some cases, individual properties that, for reasons such as innovation, embodiment of theoretical ideas or a degree of survival in their original form, encapsulate some of the special qualities of London's suburban development in a given period.

The gazetteer contains just under 300 entries across London's 29 boroughs, including the Hollies Estate in Sidcup, Fitzroy Park in Camden and Ruislip Manor in Hillingdon: all thoroughly suburban in their way, no doubt, but not places that immediately spring to mind when I think of the London suburbs, which, of course is part of their, and that book's, appeal.

I make no claims to having an encyclopedic knowledge of London or its suburbs. I am always willing to be educated. For instance, before I started writing this book I had heard of, but knew next to nothing about, Bedford Park in West London.

Before Letchworth Garden City, before Hampstead Garden Suburb, there was Bedford Park, a garden suburb by any other name, and by some reckonings the first: work began there in 1875. And whereas Letchworth Garden City was built by a visionary, and whereas Hampstead Garden Suburb was built by a social reformer, Bedford Park was built by a slightly dodgy property developer named Jonathan Carr.

He bought twenty-four acres of land from his father-in-law: a nice way to do business. It was a desirable plot just north of Turnham Green Tube station, which had opened in 1869. Carr commissioned E. W. Godwin to design houses for him. Godwin was a leading light in the Aesthetic Movement, a movement well known enough to be mocked by Gilbert and Sullivan in *Patience*, but Godwin and Carr fell out and Norman Shaw became Godwin's replacement. Shaw too eventually fell out

with Carr, but nevertheless, in due course, 365 properties were
built, some of them with artists' studios, thereby establishing
Bedford Park's reputation as an *arty* suburb.

Carr also had a well-connected brother, J. Comyns Carr, who
was a director of the Grosvenor Gallery in Bond Street. The
gallery showed 'radical' works by the Pre-Raphaelites, Rossetti,
Burne-Jones and Walter Crane, as well as Alma-Tadema and
Whistler. It all ended in tears at the gallery when Comyns fell
out with the owners – falling out seems to have been a family
trait – but he simply started a new gallery of his own, called
the New Gallery. Along the way he recommended Bedford
Park to his aesthetic friends and some of them moved in, further reinforcing its status as a Bohemian enclave. W.B. Yeats
lived there, with his father and brother, so did the playwright
Arthur Wing Pinero, and it was fashionable enough to have a
satirical (and fairly feeble) poem written about it, 'The Ballad
of Bedford Park', published in the *St James's Gazette* in 1881.
One verse runs:

> Now he who loves aesthetic cheer
> And does not mind the damp
> May come and read Rossetti here
> By a Japanese-y lamp.

Bedford Park also has some fame as the fictional Saffron Park
in G.K. Chesterton's *The Man Who Was Thursday* (1903): it's
where Lucian Gregory the 'anarchistic poet' lives. It was also, a
good many decades later, the real-world home of Richard Briers,
'Mr Suburbia' in the eyes of many sitcom enthusiasts. It seemed
a good place to go on a field trip.

As I walked from the station I quickly came face to face
with an information board, not far from the big local church,
St Michael and All Saints, again designed by Norman Shaw,
telling me that Bedford Park was described by John Betjeman

in 1960 as 'the most significant suburb built in the last century, probably the most significant in the Western world'. Betjeman seems to have been quite promiscuous with his praise for suburbs, although you can't help noticing his use of the word 'probably'.

The board also says the houses were designed 'in the Queen Anne style', with which Norman Shaw was closely associated, although given when the suburb was built, the term might more properly be Queen Anne Revival: characterised by steep roofs, usually with gables and dormers, fancy red brickwork, hanging tiles, lots of complicated chimneys, oriel windows, ornate porches. All these can be found in Bedford Park today, though I didn't see anything with the full-on haunted-house look that features in the American version of Queen Anne, and equally Bedford Park also contains some rows of modest terraced houses.

The London Encyclopaedia (1983 and onwards) edited by Ben Weinreb and Christopher Hibbert, undercuts whatever claims Bedford Park might have for architectural purity. It tells us that although Godwin and Shaw contributed their designs, they didn't supervise the building work. 'The greater part of the estate was built by jobbing builders who used bits of designs or ignored them altogether.' Those jobbing builders again: though they were presumably the guys responsible for those perfectly decent terraced houses.

On the map, Bedford Park looks to have a triangular, vaguely Christmas-tree shape, with The Avenue running up through the middle of it like a trunk, and roads off to the sides like branches. Most, but not all of this is conservation area. The top of the tree, as it were, is outside the conservation boundary. On the map this boundary is perfectly clear, though far less so on the ground. The suburban explorer, that would be me, finds it easy to wander outside the real or imagined boundaries and end up in an industrial bit of Acton.

I was walking without any great purpose, observing the 'good old' English names of the roads, Blenheim, Marlborough, Vanbrugh, Fielding, Flanders, and it was easy to get lost, but it was hard to stay lost. Just by meandering I would find myself back in some place that I recognised, though admittedly I did use interesting old cars parked in the streets as markers, since the cars were often more distinctive than the houses.

As so often, I was fascinated by the odd combination of architectural similarity and diversity. The original builders had done a certain amount to make the houses look individual and then, as ever, the inhabitants had taken it that bit further. I spotted two houses with ornate porches that had surely started out looking identical, but one had been left in its original red brick, while the other appeared to have been given a coat of plaster and then painted gleaming white. There was a stretch of houses with pronounced half-timbered gables, on which were simple wooden beams, with a plaster plaque in the centre, but again no two were exactly alike. Sometimes the wooden beams were straight and square on, but sometimes there were zesty diagonals, and those central plaques came in various shapes, some square, some round, some triangular, and one or two had been painted so that the overall effect was like the insignia of some secret organisation.

There were also a few brand-new, architecturally interesting, houses that had been shoe-horned in here and there. The best of these made little attempt to match the original style of the suburb and yet to my eye they didn't look out of place: all big windows, slate-grey brick, asymmetrical angles. In a conservation area this seemed somehow cheering and subversive. But I was worried about a few of the trees. Section 211 of the Town and Country Planning Act 1990, by which conservation areas live and die, states 'all trees in the conservation area are protected by law. It is an offence deliberately to damage or destroy a tree by cutting down, topping, lopping, uprooting or by any other

means without permission from the local planning authority ...
Six weeks' notice must be given before any work is started.'
Notwithstanding I did see some sickly looking trees that had been
severely hacked back, presumably with permission, and there
were some huge pieces of tree trunk lying around the path that
went up through the park at the top end of the suburb, though
probably these were located just beyond the conservation-area
boundary.

This being a garden suburb, there were of course gardens to
be looked at. They were well cared for, nothing very eccentric,
nothing kitsch that I could see, but there were some interesting
plantings including big olive trees, severely clipped hedges,
lollypop topiary, and one terraced house had its small front
garden absolutely full of planters and window boxes containing
carefully labelled bulbs: crocus yellow, crocus striped, crocus
mixed.

I also saw a surprising number of tasteful garden statues of
cats – well, three of them. And at one point I became aware
of a real cat, white, long-haired, walking very close to my feet,
not exactly trying to make friends, but quite untroubled and
unthreatened by me. I've concluded that it's a measure, perhaps a signifier, of a certain kind of English suburb that you
see cats wandering around freely at any time of day. This is a
high-risk feline activity I'd think, and a good few of these cats
have missing ears or shortened tails, though this white one in
Bedford Park seemed entirely intact. Now, I like cats well enough
but I don't like *cute* cats and there was nothing remotely cute
about the one by my feet. He didn't just look like the kind of
cat that the evil genius dandles on his knee, this cat looked
like an evil genius in his own right. Suburbia is a great place
for an evil genius to go into hiding and lie low, just like an
anarchist poet.

Unlike Hampstead Garden Suburb, Bedford Park did feel
properly like London. Some parts of it were very fancy, some not

really very fancy at all, though none of it looked cheap, because
nowhere in London is. And unlike Hampstead Garden Suburb
there were businesses there: a Polish shop and a Buddhist Vihara
on The Avenue, for instance. There was a pub, The Tabard, also
designed by Norman Shaw, with some very fine William de
Morgan tiles in the interior. When I went in and strolled up to the
bar, the barman asked me if I was a member of CAMRA. I was
not. I'd have got a discount if I had been. When my fish-finger
sandwich arrived it came accompanied by tiny Union Jack on
a miniature, free-standing flagpole.

Jonathan Carr's concept for Bedford Park did contain a certain
amount of idealism along with a desire to make money, and
perhaps we should be grateful for that. Suburban property
development that's driven by anything other than the profit
motive is to be cherished. But just occasionally suburbs are built
as part of a war effort. I went for another field trip, a suburban
walk between two such suburbs: from Aeroville to Roe Green
Village, both in northwest London. If you've never heard these
names, that's not at all surprising.

As we've seen, it wasn't until after 1918 that central government got seriously involved with building what we would now
call social housing. However, towards the end of World War I,
the Ministry of Works supervised the building of quite a few
estates, in effect suburbs, for workers employed in the aircraft
and munitions industries. These were inevitably on the outskirts
of London, south and north, because that's where the airfields
and factories were.

Frank Baines, an architect in his own right, later knighted
and after 1920 head of the Office of Works, supervised the whole
of this wartime building programme, including the Well Hall
estate in Eltham for employees at Woolwich Arsenal. Aeroville,
situated more or less in Colindale, is much less well known. It
was designed by the architect Herbert Matthews for workers

at the Grahame-White aircraft factory in Hendon. Plans were drawn up in 1917, but today nobody seems very certain whether work actually started before the end of hostilities. In any case, only part of the proposed scheme was ever finished.

Pevsner says of Aeroville, 'A delightful formal square of terraced Neo-Georgian cottages for 300 employees of Hendon Aerodrome.' That number seems too high, given the size of the place – it is just one square – but only a fool would argue with Pevsner, who then adds, more reliably, 'Mansard roofs with pedimented dormers. Doric colonnades to the side flanking the approach and to the centre opposite.' All of which is perfectly true.

The square must have looked grander in its early days than it does now. There's still some grass, but much of the central open space is now used as a car park. It had snowed the day before I went there, and the orientation of the buildings meant that half the square was in sunshine, half in shade, so that snow remained unthawed on the ground of the shady side.

The living accommodation is a combination of houses and flats. Entrances to the flats are discreetly placed around the back, out of sight from the square, but for the house dwellers, all the front doors open on to the square, which must mean that everybody is aware of everybody else's comings and goings, which I suppose is always a feature of a certain kind of suburbia, but seldom do suburbanites have so many front doors to keep an eye on.

Herbert Matthews was quite a guy – as well being an archi-tect, he was also one of the founders of Aerofilms, the first commercial company that took aerial photographs to order. Their archive runs to millions of images. They also published postcards. Below is a postcard of Roe Green Village, which was my next port of suburban call, an easy walk from Aeroville, close to Kingsbury, a place largely famous as the one time home of Oliver Goldsmith.

ROE GREEN *from the Air*

Roe Green Village was again built by the Ministry of Works, between 1917 and 1919, this time for workers at Airco, the Aircraft Manufacturing Company: 250 houses and flats, an inn, six shops and a doctor's house. At the time I was there, the pub had been turned into a house and was up for sale. There was no sign of any shops. It all felt very sedate and posh.

Frank Baines didn't just supervise the design of Roe Green, as he had that of Aeroville, here he did the design himself. He was besotted with the location – 'one of the most rural and charming within a radius of eight miles of Charing Cross … amidst pastures and noble oaks such as one associates with the west country. To preserve the beauties of the countryside was the architect's first endeavour, and the plan has been so laid that only one tree was sacrificed.'

He may have overstated the beauties of the site, but he was surely right to spare the trees, and his final design isn't bad at all. The whole place is staggeringly elegant for a government-built suburb, or a government-built anything, especially considering it was created while there was a war on. Today it's a conservation area, naturally, and has been since 1968. It's said, by some to be 'the jewel in the crown' of Brent Council, who refer to it as a garden village rather than a garden suburb. This seems to me, at best, dubious. Are there any villages that don't have gardens? And what's so great about being a village as opposed to a suburb? I mean, haven't we've all seen *Village of the Damned*?

Pevsner again:

> The theme continued the 'virtuoso-picturesque' mode established at Well Hall, Eltham in 1915, albeit in a rather more restrained manner. 250 Dwellings, planned at garden-suburb densities (about eleven to the acre) and laid out around the village green. Forty per cent were not houses but 'cottage flats', built in two-storey blocks resembling ordinary cottages in appearance.

Flats pretending to be cottages, a suburb pretending to be a village. Wouldn't it have been better if all concerned had just said 'We're building a really great suburb; deal with it'?

One of the most intriguing things I saw in Roe Green Village was another bit of pretence, and it was down at ground level: some letters set into a paving slab, part of the pavement, spelling out the words Aberdeen Adamant. I had never heard of that but I've discovered it's a kind faux granite, Aberdeen being famous for its real granite. The Adamant is made from chips of quarried granite set in a matrix of concrete to form a paving stone, very much the same method as is used to make the stars on the Hollywood Walk of Fame. From a London suburb to Hollywood (which is a suburb, if you ask me), from, say, Woodford to Long Beach, California – it's not as far as you might think.

There are many reasons for making a field trip to Woodford in northeast London, Borough of Redbridge. The place has all kinds of historical and cultural associations, not all of them suburban. William Morris lived there as a boy, in two different locations. Sylvia Pankhurst lived there 'in sin' with an anarchist (yes, there are a surprising number of them in suburbia), an Italian named Silvia Corio, in a house they renamed Red Cottage in case anybody doubted their political affiliations.

Woodford has a green with a statue of Winston Churchill and a memorial obelisk. It's still home to the Woodford Green Cricket Club, the second oldest cricket club in the world, founded in 1735. There's Hurst House, known for a long time as 'The Naked Beauty' until it was converted into a school. There's the former home of Clement Attlee.

And there's plenty about Woodford that is thoroughly, quint-essentially, suburban. The process began in 1856 when a railway line opened between Stratford and Loughton. There were two stations: George Lane, and the gloriously named Snakes Lane. The process of suburbanisation accelerated between the wars when the Central Line extended as far as Epping. It became and remains a desirable and expensive bit of suburbia.

Walking the streets, you see long rows of very similar, though as ever not quite identical, houses, many of them grand and expensive, some rather modest. There are hints of Arts and Crafts: steep roofs, stained glass in the front doors, leaded glass in the bay windows. I spotted a garage with crenellations, a popular suburban trope in itself, some serious topiary, a house with petrol pumps and an Aston Martin in the driveway.

I took all this in, and appreciated it, but my main reason for being in Woodford was to see the house where the novelist James Hilton had lived. I had a theory about James Hilton. He's best known for the novel *Lost Horizon* (1933) which he wrote while he was living in Oak Hill Gardens, which was actually part of Walthamstow at the time, though is now safely within the boundaries of Woodford. He was still living in that house when he wrote his other greatest hit *Goodbye, Mr Chips* (1939).

I suspect that fewer and fewer people are familiar with *Lost Horizon* these days, but everybody's heard of Shangri-La, even if they don't know exactly what it is. There was the girl group the Shangri-Las. and Ray Davies of the Kinks wrote a song titled 'Shangri-La'. It's on the concept album *Arthur (Or the Decline and Fall of the British Empire)* (1969); it's the name of Arthur's house,

> Now that you've found your paradise
> This is your kingdom to command
> You can go outside and polish your car
> Or sit by the fire in your Shangri-La.

However, the Shangri-La of Hilton's novel is not a suburban house but a mythical Tibetan kingdom, where people live to an unheard of old age, though of course there are complications, otherwise there wouldn't be a novel. *Lost Horizon* is still a surprisingly readable book and it seems extremely modern in some respects, though the sexual politics are inevitably a bit dodgy. A plane crashes in the impenetrable mountains of Tibet, and the passengers are rescued by the inhabitants of a lamasery in Shangri-La, who take them in and educate them about the wonders of the place. Initially very impressed, the plane-crash survivors before long feel the need to escape and get back to their real lives.

The film is probably better known than the book. Directed by Frank Capra, starring Ronald Coleman, it is ruthlessly unfaithful to the original – the female missionary from the novel becomes a floozy, the hero Conway suddenly has a brother, and Edward Everett Horton pops up as a palaeontologist. There was a 1973 remake, a musical, starring Peter Finch and Liv Ullman. I'm sure somebody, somewhere has watched it from beginning to end, but I've never encountered such a brave soul.

The book was written in the winter of 1932 when Hilton might already have suspected that things were looking bleak for the world, even from a suburban outpost in Oak Hill Gardens.

Perhaps he anticipated a global conflict, and he imagined a place where a small pocket of civilisation could survive however bad things got.

I haven't been able to find any comments Hilton made about his London neighbourhood, but his description of Shangri-La sounds strangely like a version of Middle England. Chang, a postulant at the lamasery, who speaks excellent if stilted English, explains how things are in Shangri-La: 'If I were to put it into a very few words, my dear sir, I should say that our prevalent belief is in moderation. We inculcate the virtue of avoiding excesses of all kinds – even including, if you will pardon the paradox, excess of virtue itself ... And I think I can claim that our people are moderately sober, moderately chaste and moderately honest.' This sounds more like a relaxed Church of England vicar than a Tibetan lama, but perhaps the two aren't so very different. Chang also describes the lack of crime in Shangri-La, attributing it partly to the fact that only serious things are considered crimes and 'partly because everyone enjoyed a sufficiency of everything he could reasonably desire'.

You may think the book is starting to go off the rails a bit when Chang says, 'You English inculcate the same feeling in your public schools,' but then there's a wonderful swerve, as he continues, 'but not I fear for the same things. The inhabitants of our valley, for instance feel that it is "not done" to be inhospitable to strangers, to dispute acrimoniously, or to strive for priority amongst one another. The idea of enjoying what your English headmasters call the mimic warfare of the playing field would seem to them entirely barbarous, indeed, a sheer wanton simulation of all the lower instincts.' From which I think we might infer that Hilton wasn't good at sports.

It wasn't hard to find Hilton's house. It was unexceptional in certain respects, a two-storey, semi-detached house, with cream-coloured rendering and a half-timbered gable, in a street of similar houses, but the presence of a blue plaque was the giveaway.

Whoever lives in the house now isn't shy about expressing their personality. There was a skeleton hanging in the front window, which could have been a leftover from Halloween but since my visit there was in February the inhabitants obviously liked having it around.

After his success as a novelist, Hilton became even more successful as a Hollywood screenwriter and went to live in California full time, where he subsequently won an Oscar for the script of *Mrs Miniver* (1942), which is about how ordinary people cope in a time of war, though it isn't set in suburbia. But interestingly (to me) he didn't live in Beverley Hills or Malibu or any of the places where so many successful screenwriters settle; for the last ten years of his life (he died youngish, aged 54) he lived in Long Beach, in a bungalow on Argonne Avenue. I've walked and driven around Long Beach, though not along Argonne Street, and it's a very different kind of suburbia from Woodford (or Walthamstow), but it's still recognisably a member of the species.

Even at the time it evidently seemed an odd place for an Oscar winner to make his home, and Hilton was happy to explain in an interview: 'I want to live in America. I want to write about it. You can't get the feel of the country from Hollywood, so I came to Long Beach.'

Perhaps the same could be said about England and Woodford. Neither Woodford nor Long Beach is one hundred per cent typical of its respective country but they're both conventional enough, respectable, unflashy, to an extent anonymous. They don't pretend to be anything they're not, but there may well be wild flights of imagination, invention and fantasy going on behind the locked front doors.

Depending on how you look at it, Hilton either came a long way or he didn't come very far at all, from one suburb to another, from the outskirts of London to the outskirts of Los Angeles. His horizon wasn't so lost, after all, and certainly it

wasn't so very distant. If it suited your thesis, you could argue
that the suburbs, whether English or American, were his idea
of Shangri-La.

14

Los Angeles, the Penultimate Suburb

There's a convincing argument to be made that Los Angeles is the most suburban city on earth. As you fly in and make a circling approach to LAX Airport, you can look down and see hundreds of thousands, possibly millions of individual homes, each in its own patch of land, arranged geometrically along gridded, orderly streets. I think it looks fantastic. On the ground this vision still applies, and even in some of the roughest, toughest areas you'll find detached one-family houses, with their own reasonably-sized garden, a garage and driveway. The house will be frayed at the edges, the cars in the drive won't be new, the garden may be neglected, there may well be a sagging chain-link fence around the whole thing, but visually the neighbourhood suggests careworn suburbia rather than desperate 'mean streets'.

This may look like the very definition of sprawl, although as mentioned earlier there is no universal definition of that troubling term. By certain standards however, chiefly those of population density, Los Angeles scarcely sprawls at all. Yes, its population is spread out over many, many square miles but in fact the city's overall population density, and the density of LA's suburbs, is in fact very high, higher than the overall population density of New York, San Francisco or Chicago. That's because LA's population is very evenly distributed so that the difference between the density of inner city (a minor phenomenon in LA) and suburb is negligible. This won't seem like much consolation when you're stuck in your car during a two-hour commute, but it does mean that when you get home you'll have your house, your castle, your own patch of outdoor space.

Things are now changing and that change happened even as I lived in LA. Sprawl became an ever dirtier word. Suburban life, single-family homes, were increasingly perceived as wasteful and environmentally damaging. Apartment buildings, some much higher-rise than others, are going up all over the city. Even so it will be a good long time before LA, overall, becomes less than suburban. I don't know if that's a shame or not. I was pretty content with the suburban life I lived there for fifteen years, until the day I wasn't.

The important thing to know about my move to Los Angeles is that it had nothing whatsoever to do with trying to 'get into' the movies. I like movies, I like watching them, I like the gossip and the craft, even some of the stars and directors, and I did have a distant, nodding acquaintance with one or two movie producers who'd bought the movie rights to a few of my novels. One of them,* against all my expectations, even got made, but I didn't write the script and I never wanted to be a scriptwriter.

---

* *Permanent Vacation* (2009), based on my novel *What We Did on Our Holidays*, directed by Scott Peake, with a movie-stealing performance by David Carradine. It is, I think you'd have to say, a movie about a suburbanite who goes rogue.

I was happy enough to be an observer of the 'industry' but I had no desire to be part of it. I was a writer of novels and books of non-fiction, and that was precisely what I wanted to be. I told myself that being an LA-based writer who didn't write movies and who didn't *want* to write movies was a very healthy state of affairs. I would be a rarity, and I would keep my sanity when those around me went crazy because of notes from the studios and demands from the lead actors.

I moved to LA for what struck me at the time as the best of all possible reasons: because of a woman. My then girlfriend, later my wife, lived in Brooklyn, New York, and I lived in Maida Vale, London. We had a transatlantic relationship that had already lasted for five years, and although that kind of relationship comes with some obvious difficulties, it was working pretty well, and we wanted it to continue. However, when my girlfriend's book publishing job gave her the opportunity to live and work in Los Angeles, it was clear that a long-distance relationship that regularly involved not just crossing the Atlantic but the whole of the continental United States as well, was going to be just too difficult. So why didn't I move to LA as well? I could write anywhere so why not there? We'd find a place to live, probably we'd get married, I'd get my green card, and all would be well. Most of this did in fact happen.

I was already a serious Angelenophile. I'd been there a good few times, mostly as a tourist, a couple of times on working holidays. I'd seen the films, I'd seen the photographs. I'd read my Chandler, my Rayner Banham, my Nathanael West. I'd even read Mike Davis's *City of Quartz* (1990), subtitled 'Excavating the Future of Los Angeles'. The book portrays the city as a set of discrete, dystopian enclaves, each the territory of a warring tribe. The fact that some of these enclaves are in fact very expensive and exclusive gated suburbs would appear, in Davis's account, to be both the symptom and the disease.

He writes:

The discarded Joshua trees, the profligate waste of water, the claustrophobic walls, and the ridiculous names are as much a polemic against incipient urbanism as they are an assault on the endangered wilderness. The *eutopic* (literally no-place) logic of their subdivisions, in sterilized sites stripped bare of nature and history, masterplanned only for privatized family consumption, evokes much of the past evolution of tract-house Southern California. But the developers are not just repackaging myth (the good life in the suburbs) for the next generation; they are also pandering to a new, burgeoning fear of the city.

The idea that LA was part police state, part ungovernable chaos was scary, of course, but it was also madly appealing in a 'living on the edge', post-*Blade Runner* kind of way. If you could survive there, you could survive anywhere. It would be like living in the suburbs of Gomorrah. And off we went.

I had few expectations of how or where we might live in Los Angeles. My girlfriend and I were long-time flat or apartment dwellers. On the occasions that we'd visited LA together we'd looked, out of curiosity, at local real-estate ads, since they're everywhere, and it appeared that LA was cheaper than either London or New York. We could see possibilities. It looked like we might be able to own a little house, a bungalow, a unit, with a garden, a driveway, a garage; yes, something very suburban. I admit this had its appeal.

We began by renting a small place in Silver Lake and spent weekends looking at properties to buy, even as it seemed that prices were rising day by day. Seeing how other people live is always fascinating, and in LA there were specific, local fascinations. We went to view a house that had been clad entirely in black volcanic rock. It was on an otherwise unremarkable, middle-class suburban street close to Wilshire Boulevard. It had been owned by a local eccentric known variously around the neighbourhood as the Witch of Wilshire, the Moon Lady, the Black Widow and most tellingly of all as the Lava Lady. The house wasn't expensive, and for a moment we did consider it, but in the end we weren't brave enough to take on a house that was coated in pumice.

We saw a bungalow in Beachwood Canyon with a den in the back yard, a kind of cave that had been excavated out of the rock that rose up at the end of the garden. The seller said this was where 'the drummer from the Beach Boys' had practised. I didn't argue but I found it hard to believe that Dennis Wilson had ever practised, or needed to practise, in a hollowed-out den. True, after his death, the Beach Boys had employed other drummers, but it seemed to me that anyone who was in line to play drums with the Beach Boys would have had a much more sophisticated practice studio.

We looked at a 1960s house that had been built with a stereo (perhaps more properly a gramophone, possibly a radiogram) in an alcove in the living room, with wires that ran inside the walls to loud-speakers in every room. We learned that a couple of avocado trees in a garden could add an exorbitant premium to the price of a property. We observed all the trouble that some people had gone to in order to shoehorn a tiny swimming pool into their back yard. We saw how many residents had artistic aspirations, or possibly even careers, and had built a writer's hut, an art studio or a recording studio in a corner of their plot.

And of course we weren't very good at understanding or sussing out the neighbourhoods. They all looked pretty good to us. A realtor showed us a bungalow just off Hollywood Boulevard and it struck us as a possibility, but as we came out and were talking positively about it, the realtor looked at us sadly, a couple of rubes, and said, 'Nah, you people wouldn't want to be here at night.' We took his word for it.

But the fact was, for all their variety, the majority of the places we looked at turned out to be smallish, detached suburban

houses, with the usual trappings and trimmings. In many ways
these were more than we needed, more than we were looking for,
but in some way, without having sought it out, we were generally
looking at versions of the American suburban dream. Some of
these houses we could afford, some we couldn't. Some we knew
just weren't for us. But at a certain point we realised, and possibly
we should have known it all along, given our price range, that
we were generally looking at the cheap, somewhat quirky house
on the expensive street. This hadn't been our intention, but we
didn't object, and in any case it seemed preferable to living in
the expensive house on the cheap street.

And so it was that we went to look at a geodesic dome,
located on what I came to describe as the lower slopes of the
Hollywood Hills, although, depending on whom you're trying
to impress, or not impress, it could have been said to be in Los
Feliz or East Hollywood or The Oaks.

I know that people tend to think that geodesic domes are
homes for hippies, preferably located in the desert or up in the
mountains surrounded by pines, but this was a *suburban* geodesic
dome, built in the 1980s by a schoolteacher who'd inherited a plot
of land from his mother. He and his Korean wife were moving
out and downsizing because of poor health. The dome was tucked
into a hillside, close to other houses but screened from them by
the lie of the land and by some strategically placed trees.

We didn't leap immediately. I'd always liked the look and
the concept of the geodesic dome, popularised though by no
means invented by Buckminster Fuller. They provided lots of
space, enclosed by the minimum amount of materials. I can't say
I'd ever had an overwhelming ambition to live in one, but the
place we saw was attractive and appealing, with plenty of space,
even if the décor was a bit tired and 1980s (acres of aquamarine
carpet, though we got rid of that), and it had a dodgy-looking
roof that had to be replaced, but what clinched it, and maybe
this isn't the best reason for buying a house, though there are

surely worse ones, I decided I didn't want to be the guy who goes around saying, 'We almost lived in a geodesic dome, you know.' I wanted to be able to say, 'I once lived in a geodesic dome,' whatever the final outcome. We made an offer, we got a mortgage, we were in business.

While we were waiting for the legalities to be finalised, we decided to take a walk around the neighbourhood one Saturday afternoon to get a feel of the area, and if the opportunity arose we'd speak to one or two of the neighbours and ask what it was like to live there. We saw very few people. We thought some were definitely at home, but they were hidden behind their gates, walls, fences and hedges. The notion that the front garden is for others, the back garden for yourself, really doesn't apply in most of LA. There are exceptions, but in general all the garden is all for you, and the less passers-by can see of it the better. The property section of the *LA Times* regularly contains ads for landscape nurseries offering 'Hollywood hedges' – fully grown tress, generally cedars or cypresses, twenty or thirty feet high, that can be trucked in and installed in a couple of days to provide swift seclusion: 'Instantly block those nosy neighbors and unsightly views!'

At last we did see a man working in one of the gardens, and in our naive way we said hello and asked, 'Do you live here?' The look he gave us contained mostly sneering contempt, though perhaps there was also a hint of pity for our lack of nous. Or perhaps he thought we were mocking him. The man was Hispanic and as we realised after we'd moved in, as anybody in Los Angeles would know, if you see a Hispanic man working in a garden in the Hollywood Hills, even on the lower slopes, he is not the owner of the house, he's the gardener. And that was the case here. We had a lot of learn.

And sure, no point denying it, we lived in a very white neighbourhood. A Black guy lived across the street for a while. He had a big four-wheel drive with a very loud sound system, but none of the neighbours treated him any differently from anybody else, any differently from the way they treated each other. They said hello if they had occasion to, but those occasions were few and far between.

For what it's worth, our house had a deed on the land, unenforceable and dating from the 1930s, forbidding the sale of the land to 'Hindus'. I always assumed this was code for 'Indians', but I was never completely sure. I certainly don't think it was an indication that every other religious group would be welcomed with open arms. I think it was taken for granted that Black and Southeast Asian people, whatever their religion, were never going to be able to afford to buy the land and live there, so that problem didn't arise. But there was just a chance that those enterprising Hindus from Bombay or Calcutta might have the money to be able to buy into Hollywood. That apparently had to be nipped in the bud.

Once we moved into the house and I'd started working on the garden – I'd got to the stage in life when I enjoyed gardening – I saw that I was the only person in the entire street who did his own gardening. Everybody else employed teams of Mexicans who came once a week and used deafening leaf blowers. If this singled me out as some weird English mad dog, nobody ever said so to my face, but then none of the neighbours ever talked to me much at all. They probably just thought I was poor and eccentric. They weren't entirely wrong.

I enjoyed making a new garden, and on occasions we did have to employ a professional, somebody who was handy with a chainsaw, to clear scrub or cut down tree branches that hung too close to the house. This was usually in response to an annual letter from the city telling us to make the garden safe for fire season. Too much scrub produces kindling for fires in the hills. If we hadn't had the work done, we'd have got a fine and then the authorities would have sent in a contractor to do the work at local government rates, and sent us an inflated bill for the work.

It never got that far: we really didn't want to get fined, and we definitely didn't want our house to go up in flames.

People in LA do put a lot of thought and money into their gardens. The thought may be that of a professional landscaper, the money will usually be their own, but the labour will most likely be other people's. There are palm trees of course, sometimes giant cacti, succulents, agaves, euphorbia, things that don't need a lot of water, that's the current recommendation, which I was happy to accept, although there remains another category of garden that still requires huge amounts of watering and irrigation. These gardens are frowned upon by environmentalists, but oddly enough this has a limited effect on certain wealthy LA types.

When the time came for the unhappy divorce and I had to move out, saying goodbye to the garden upset me far more than saying goodbye to the house. A small and ignoble part of me did think about razing the garden, hacking it all down, spraying it with weedkiller, spreading salt all over the ground to piss off my wife, but no, I didn't do that. I was a distraught, spurned husband, not a maniac or a monster.

If we think of a suburb as being rows and grids of more or less identical houses, then the Hollywood Hills refuse to conform. Here every house is different from its neighbour. Some of them are unspectacular, and are indeed the kind of house you might find in any American suburb of a certain era, low-rise, detached, single-family tract houses, but others break the mould completely. They can be quite ugly: out-of-place faux chateaux, haciendas or castles. There are quite a few houses known locally as Arts and Crafts, though I don't think William Morris would have recognised them as such. Some are mid-century, some ultra-modern.

Some are spectacularly original, designed by 'name' archi-tects, sometimes owned by people who are names in the movie industry, but they sit cheek by jowl with perfectly ordinary, much smaller properties, the grand and the ordinary together in a kind of harmony, side by side. I tend to think this is a good thing.

Before I lived in Los Angeles I'd read books about LA architecture, looked at photographs of buildings by the likes of Frank Lloyd Wright and his son Lloyd Wright, by Gregory Ain, Richard Neutra, Rudolph Schindler, and they appeared to be surrounded by masses of empty space, but this was often a trick of the photographer. When I went on my field trips to look at these architectural gems they'd often be in surprisingly ordinary suburban neighbourhoods, tucked in between perfectly mundane houses and bungalows. At first this was surprising and disappointing, but I quickly got used to it, and I came to appreciate how the grand and the ordinary could be encompassed in a single neighbourhood, in a single frame.

Change and development were always conspicuous in the neighbourhood where we lived, houses being worked on, extended, given new roofs, new patios, just like in any suburban neighbourhood. But sometimes it was far more extreme than that, not just a matter of an upgrade, an extension or a granny flat above the garage. Here you'd see complete transformations, not 'tear downs' as they're called in those parts, not demolitions and rebuilding from scratch, because that involved all kinds of difficulties with planning and permits. But, for example, there was a small one-storey house nearby, a bungalow essentially, that was stripped down to the studs, leaving just a roofless, wall-less, wooden frame, and then it was rebuilt to look nothing remotely like a bungalow but rather like a very stylish, and currently very fashionable, minimalist, Brutalist concrete block. It looked great to my eyes, but you could question its authenticity. Many would also question whether it belonged in suburbia; no doubt many also felt that way about a geodesic dome.

One of the attractions of living in Los Angeles, as far as I was concerned, was that you could get in your car, drive due east along the freeway, and on a good day, depending on the traffic, and in Southern California everything always depends on the traffic, you could be in the Mojave Desert in a couple of hours.

Naturally we think of the desert as being all about space, emptiness, wildness, big skies, isolation, the absence of humanity, but if you find yourself staying in the Travelodge in Yucca Valley, as I regularly did, you can look out of your window and see that suburban developments have been built right up to the parking lot of the motel. The desert has been eaten up and covered up, divided into generously sized plots on which have been built large single-storey houses, often with double or triple garages. The desert has been turned into suburbia.

I was, and am, essentially unhappy and uncomfortable with this, just like any desert lover. The desert should be the desert. But there were occasions when I woke up early in the motel room and rather than getting into the Jeep and driving to some remote part of the desert for an early-morning walk, I simply went on foot and explored this desert suburb.

Needless to say, this was not the pure desert experience that I was usually looking for, but I think you can be too precious about these things, and it was definitely *some* form of desert experience. I believe in looking at what's there rather than at what's not, and this was a version of suburbia I'd never seen before. It was a golden opportunity.

The houses in this suburb were not the 'home in the desert' as most people, myself included, would generally conceive of it. The more usual image is of a wooden or cinderblock shack down a dirt road, not necessarily having electricity or water, and surrounded by 5 or 10 acres of raw desert, the next neighbour more than yelling distance away.

And when my wife told me our marriage was unnegotiably over, I did think, briefly, OK, I'll go and move into one of those desert shacks, become a deracinated Englishman gone native in the desert. But by then I was seeing a therapist (yes, I had gone a little bit Hollywood) and he said, and it came as no great surprise, that since I was feeling lonely, depressed and isolated, it really wouldn't be good for my mental health to isolate myself further by holing up in a desert shack. And even if I'd moved into a house in desert suburbia, I probably wouldn't have felt much less isolated. I certainly didn't imagine I'd fit in, although since I never put it to the test, I could have been wrong about that.

Walk out of the Travelodge and you're in Camino Del Cielo Drive. The street names, always a powerful indication of developers' intentions, if not of their achievements, honour a Spanish heritage, despite there being a much earlier Native American one in that area. So the streets are not called streets. They're mostly named trails, Martinez Trail, Benecia Trail, San Remo, El Prado, Cardillo.

The houses that have been built here and in other subdivisions near by are not *of* the desert and they don't exactly blend in with the landscape; in a sense they look like the kind of houses that, with exceptions, might be built anywhere in Southern California, perhaps anywhere in America, although not every house in America has a couple of giant Joshua trees growing in their front yard. Those trees were not, *pace* Mike Davis, 'discarded'.

Some of the houses look as though they've been dropped into the middle of a cactus forest, with towering columns, spikes and paddles lining the paths and driveways and pressing up against the windows. Those were the ones I liked best. Other houses looked as though they'd been built on a flat, scoured, largely featureless bit of scrub and sand, and a few cacti and succulents had been left, or possibly planted as landscaping, to fit in with the rest of the neighbourhood.

There were elements of Hispanic, or at least faux Hispanic, architecture: red-tiled roofs, Mission-style arches on porches and gates. A few even show some mid-century modern influence:

flat roofs, angled buttresses, some post and beam, but in general the houses are long and low, the roofs broad and shallow. Some of the walls are brick, but most are coated in pale earth-coloured rendering or stucco, and one or two look like they're made of some prefabricated, metallic substance. As I walked around I saw wildlife – a lot of jack rabbits, a few roadrunners, flocks of desert quail. I enjoyed that. It confirmed the sense of being in the desert but it didn't make the overall effect any less suburban.

The few people I met as I walked seemed friendly enough, and as ever nobody asked me my business. Maybe it was obvious that I was a tourist staying at the motel. A few looked like retirees, but many seemed like working family men, setting off to do a day's hard labour. It seemed to me they weren't leading such a bad life.

This was comparatively cheap housing, perhaps not as cheap as you think it ought to be, given that in the middle of summer the resident suburbanites have to endure temperatures of well over a hundred degrees Fahrenheit, but it's cheaper than the equivalent in most other parts of California. If you're earning a decent wage, these houses are comparatively affordable and you can still have enough left over for some discretionary spending on toys. That's why outside these desert houses you're likely to see a good few vehicles: one will probably be a truck, one may be a classic muscle car, there's a high probability there'll be a big luxurious camper, there very well might be a couple of trail bikes and a dune buggy. There are even a surprising number of boats – the Colorado River isn't so very far away.

The people who live here don't want the mythical desert shack, they want a three-bedroom house with a nice bit of ground they can call their own, with plenty of room for the kids, plenty of parking and garaging, and a short drive into town to the supermarket and the K-Mart. In Yucca Valley this was available and they went for it.

One morning on my walk I met an old man, by which I mean that he looked significantly older than me, and, as he appeared to be friendly and we nodded at each other, I felt able to ask, 'What's it like living here?' I suppose I imagined he'd complain about the summer heat and possibly about the winter cold, but instead he said, 'It's God's own country.' I didn't argue with him.

Now, of course there's no real argument in favour of turning the desert into a suburb. You might say it's a desecration and a despoilation and in broad, simple terms, ninety-five days out of a hundred, I'd completely agree with you. It would be far, far better if the desert were left untouched, not built on, much less suburbanised. And if the local zoning authorities in Yucca Valley had decided that the desert should remain pristine, that would have been a very good thing indeed. But they didn't. They decided to allow people to build and live in the desert. If you were a hardline urbanist you might say that building single family homes *anywhere* is wrong. And in fairness it should be said that Yucca Valley does have some apartment buildings, and like many desert communities it has its share of trailer parks, which certainly don't sprawl. The trailers are packed in there as tightly as if they were in a supermarket car park on Black Friday. Is that a better way of living? I honestly don't know. I think much must depend on who's in the trailer next door.

But sometimes I entertain the notion, part Le Corbusier, part J.G. Ballard, of a giant high-rise tower block sitting in the middle of the desert, the population densely packed inside their apartments, with the building's 'grounds' extending to thousands of square miles of untouched desert. That would be a non-suburban way of living in the Mojave. But I'm not holding my breath, and I'm pretty sure that nobody currently alive would actually want to live like that. I'm tempted to say that maybe it will become an attractive idea to future generations, but by then it might be too late: the whole of the desert could have been turned into one giant suburb by then, or maybe every suburb will have turned into a desert.

Spalding Gray's memoir/monologue *Monster in a Box* (1992) contains a telling, if overly familiar, description of a writer's life in the Hollywood Hills. 'The Monster' is the novel he's working on.

> ... I'd get up and run over to my desk and open the Monster to work on it; the sun would stream across my writing hand and relax it. And I'd follow the sun around into the living room and have a cup of coffee, and watch the sun stream through the eucalyptus trees and have another cup of coffee, and watch the sun come through the palm trees. Then follow the sun into the dining room, and watch the sun come through the dining room window and have a martini. Watch the sun set over Sunset Strip and have another martini. Why go out? Why bother? Why work on a book?

This doesn't altogether describe the life I lived in LA, but I recognise it. I worked in a basement room which did have a window on to the garden, but the sun never streamed in; I chose the room as an office for that very reason. And having some reputation as a walker, I did try to leave the house for at least an hour a day and walk somewhere, but I never thought, 'Why work on a book?' I worked all the time. I even liked to think that my walking was part of the creative process. When it comes to writing, I've always been regular and fastidious in my habits, not quite a nine-to-fiver but close enough, although, yes, when happy hour came around I did sometimes find myself, like Spalding Gray, with a martini in my hand; and it's even true that often I could see no point in bothering to go out. I had everything I needed right there in the house.

At about seven o'clock my wife would come home from work, from her 'real' job, that took her out of the house and into the world every day. I was always glad to see her, perhaps gladder than she was to see me, and of course we went out sometimes but more often than not we stayed at home.

And maybe this is an important difference between urban and suburban life. Urban life is lived far more outside the home than in it. After a day's writing in my flat in London I was always eager to get out there and *do* something, anything. I rarely felt that way in Los Angeles.

And then one day my wife announced that she didn't want to be married to me any more. This came out of the blue and as a terrible shock. I hadn't been complacent, I hadn't thought our marriage was perfect: does anyone? I thought there were one or two minor problems that we might have addressed more directly, frustrations and irritations on both sides, but I didn't think it was anything worse than that. And so the announcement was devastating. My wife said I was no fun. I was a melancholic, a depressive. I didn't and couldn't deny that – melancholia and depression have been my lifelong companions, but nevertheless my wife and I still talked a lot, laughed a lot, shared a sense of humour. Or so it seemed to me. I thought we still found each other clever and witty. I thought we were best friends. How wrong can you be? I argued that we should stay together, I thought we had too much to lose, I thought that whatever the problems we could work them out. My wife thought very differently.

We had a 'trial separation' and she went to stay in an Airbnb for a couple of weeks, while I had a miserable, lonely time in the empty marital home. When I suggested that after this separation we might have a 'trial reconciliation' she wouldn't accept that. It was all over as far as she was concerned. I also thought – Occam's razor – that she might simply have found somebody else, and as time goes by I've come to think that must have been the case, though she never said so, and if that was the case I didn't really want to know.

After much pain and misery, and a few expensive visits to the therapist, I accepted the inevitable and agreed to a divorce. You can't spend your life wanting to be with somebody who doesn't want to be with you. And in due course I headed back to England. Did I miss Los Angeles? Did I miss the city, our house, the garden, my wife, my old life? I most certainly did, and sometimes, perhaps more often than is strictly healthy, I still do. Time moves on, and in due course things hurt less than they used to, but it's not a straightforward progression. I've moved on because I had to, ended up in a new home in a small, chalet-style house in Lawford Dale, in Essex, a new life in a new suburb. Do I sometimes feel lonely, sad, bereft? Of course I do, but it's not because I'm living in suburbia.

15

The Last Suburban Walk:
An Englishman's Home is His Bunker

There's a walk I sometimes do, usually alone. I step outside my front door, take a right, another right, then a left down a pedestrian walkway between houses with wooden fences. There are bands of long grass on either side of the path, where mushrooms and fungi thrive. When I get to the bottom of the walkway I'm no longer in my suburb of Lawford Dale, though I'm still in Lawford, and I arrive at the main drag, Station Road, though I'm heading in the other direction, away from the station.

I go through, or under, a railway bridge. On the inside wall of the bridge somebody has painted, neatly but in now faded and scarcely legible words: ANOTHER RUINED LANDSCAPE, all

caps. I don't know whether this is intended to convey that the
bridge and the railway line have ruined the landscape, whether
it's the building of suburbs that's the source of ruination, or
whether it's some meta-reference to the graffito itself. It probably doesn't pay to overthink these things, but my neighbour
Dorothy, who's lived in Lawford Dale for a good long time,
tells me that when she first saw the suburb being built she
thought it looked like a blot on the landscape; she called it
Lego architecture. Now, having lived here a couple of decades,
she thinks it's Shangri-La.

After the bridge I walk alongside a small industrial estate
until I come to a marked public footpath that runs between a
facility where mini containers are stored and a yard where lorries
park, some of them with a sign on the back that reads 'Convoi
Exceptionnel'. The footpath can be very muddy depending on
the time of year and the recent weather, but I'm soon past it, and
ahead is a set of concrete steps that leads up a grassy embankment
and at the top there's a great view of the River Stour estuary.

I turn left along the path at the top of the embankment,
going slightly back on myself, making a big, horseshoe-shaped
loop. There are always dog walkers up here, who more often than
not say hello. Sometimes there are serious bird watchers too,
occasionally whole groups of them, and if they're photographers
with more camera equipment than you think they'd be able to
carry. They don't usually say anything at all. Perhaps they don't
want to scare away the birds. I like birds well enough and I can
identify the more obvious ones: swans, herons, ducks, egrets,
wild geese that I dare say sometimes fly with the moon on their
wings, but I'm not here for the wild life, I'm on my way to what
I inaccurately refer to as the Manningtree Bunker.

To be accurate it's a FW3/22 Pillbox. There are similar fortifications all over East Anglia, in fact all over the East Coast, officially called 'hardened field defences', constructed in the early
1940s in anticipation of a German invasion. Some of them are

currently right in the middle of suburbs – I could take you to
a favourite one in suburban Saxmundham, in Suffolk – though
naturally they weren't built that way. They were usually built in
fields, but after the war some of the fields were sold off and suburbs constructed on them. The pillboxes were rarely demolished
because it was just too difficult to demolish them: six-feet-thick
reinforced concrete walls were common, and perhaps they've
also been left as plain, brutal and very effective war memorials.

To get to 'my' bunker I pass under another railway bridge,
officially the River Wall Subway, this one really quite small and
narrow, barely wide enough for two pedestrians to walk through
side by side. There are more graffiti here: somebody called Arly
has been at work and somebody, perhaps even Arly, has painted
quite a decent representation of a pineapple, which I think may
be the logo for something I'm not hip enough to recognise.

And so I arrive at the pillbox. In common with all Type 22s
the ground plan is a regular hexagon, about twelve feet across,
and it has a perfectly flat roof. You can, and I do, stand on that
roof and feel above it all, even though in reality you're not above
very much. Once in a while I arrive and there's already somebody
standing where I want to stand, in which case I leave them to it.
You can't be king of the castle when there's some stranger standing
right next to you. But small groups of people have obviously
congregated there at one time or another, and left behind a silt
of beer cans, bottles and plastic wrapping on the ground around
the base of the structure. There are embrasures (that's holes to
you and me) in the concrete walls, through which rifles or light
machine guns could be fired in all directions, although the river
embankment has been built up higher than the level of the
embrasures on the northeast side, which is the direction from
which the enemy seems most likely to have come.

From the flat roof I can look back over the water at the
birds and the railway bridge and the occasional passing train,
and there's a field that usually has sheep in it but is sometimes

flooded, in which case the sheep go elsewhere. This bunker is not in suburbia, but standing there scanning the horizons you can see suburbs in pretty much every direction, orderly rows of neat and newish houses, some are more distant than others but none of them is so very far away. You can't quite see my house from here but you can certainly see my suburb. Since I'm fascinated by suburbs, there are times when I think this suburban plenitude is a good thing, other times, admittedly, when I wonder if there really needs to be so many.

A few miles up the road from where I stand on top of the pillbox, in a place called Mistley, there's a 'secret bunker' which has become the centerpiece of a brand new suburban housing development. Well, there have been recent times when the idea of living in a bunker has seemed very attractive to a lot of people. Those survivalists who build bomb-proof and people-proof shelters seemed to have a point, though whether something that would protect you from a nuclear blast would necessarily protect you from a virus is moot.

Meanwhile, in the actual suburbs, I live with the new normal which really doesn't seem so very different from the way I lived with the old normal. Even so, I seem to have a lot more time on my hands than I used to, time even to return to Gaston Bachelard's *Poetics of Space,* where I finally found a passage that seems relevant to the present suburban condition. He writes, 'the house shelters daydreaming, the house protects the dreamer, the house allows one to dream in peace.'

I think this is true, whether you're in a pandemic, in a lock-down or not, but it also raises the question of what it is that suburbanites daydream *about*. Well obviously they, we, don't all dream about the same things. No doubt new patio doors and bigger conservatories figure in some of these reveries, no doubt social justice, anti-imperialism and hopes for a better world figure in others. And some people, I'm sure, daydream about moving on, about going somewhere else, somewhere better, perhaps glossier, perhaps higher up the property ladder, to somewhere less suburban, or possibly *more* suburban. Some must dream of downsizing. Some, no doubt, must think about a worse future, not so much a daydream as a grim fantasy (which for some will become a reality) about moving into the granny flat, the retirement home, the nursing facility, the hospice.

At some time or another I have daydreamed – and fretted – about all these things, and I still regularly ask myself what I'm doing here. And I suppose the simple answer is: surviving, leading a quiet life, getting on with things, living as well as I can. Isn't that what everybody's doing? I continue to wonder, as I did earlier in this book, how long suburbs will continue to exist in their current recognisable form, and whether they deserve to, but there's no doubt that they'll outlast and outlive me. They'll still be here long after I, and all of my neighbours, have gone. Bricks and mortar are more enduring than the human presence, the human lives they contain. That's not really the subject for a daydream, more an intimation of mortality, and I suppose the suburbs are full of those too. There is a cliché that living well is the best revenge. I'd like to think that writing well is a kind of revenge too. Throughout all this I did have one small, localised, personal dream, that I'd finish my book about the suburbs. Not every dream has to crash and burn.

Acknowledgements

Many thanks to the following people who have helped me in the writing of this book, often in ways they may not have been aware of.

Caroline Gannon
Joanna Moriarty
Sue Coulbeck
Paul Spooner
Jen Pedler
Del Barrett
Anthony Miller
Tammy Fraser
Joe Zinnato
Foster Spragge
Mat Clum
Colin Marshall
Bruce Baumann
Steve Erickson
Travis Elborough
Janet Fitch
Kirsty Allison
Richard Lapper
Jonathan Taylor
Penny Hughes-Stanton
Dorothy Howe